T0384920

An Analysis of

Plato's

The Republic

James Orr

Published by Macat International Ltd
24:13 Coda Centre, 189 Munster Road, London SW6 6AW.

Distributed exclusively by Routledge
2 Park Square, Milton Park, Abingdon, Oxon OX14 4RN
711 Third Avenue, New York, NY 10017, USA

Routledge is an imprint of the Taylor & Francis Group, an informa business

www.macat.com
info@macat.com

Cataloguing in Publication Data
A catalogue record for this book is available from the British Library.
Library of Congress Cataloguing-in-Publication Data is available upon request.
Cover illustration: Etienne Gilfillan

ISBN 978-1-912303-11-3 (hardback)
ISBN 978-1-912127-87-0 (paperback)
ISBN 978-1-912281-99-2 (e-book)

Notice
The information in this book is designed to orientate readers of the work under analysis,
to elucidate and contextualise its key ideas and themes, and to aid in the development
of critical thinking skills. It is not meant to be used, nor should it be used, as a
substitute for original thinking or in place of original writing or research. References and
notes are provided for informational purposes and their presence does not constitute
endorsement of the information or opinions therein. This book is presented solely for
educational purposes. It is sold on the understanding that the publisher is not engaged
to provide any scholarly advice. The publisher has made every effort to ensure that
this book is accurate and up-to-date, but makes no warranties or representations with
regard to the completeness or reliability of the information it contains. The information
and the opinions provided herein are not guaranteed or warranted to produce particular
results and may not be suitable for students of every ability. The publisher shall not be
liable for any loss, damage or disruption arising from any errors or omissions, or from
the use of this book, including, but not limited to, special, incidental, consequential or
other damages caused, or alleged to have been caused, directly or indirectly, by the
information contained within.

CONTENTS

THE MACAT LIBRARY

The Macat Library is a series of unique academic explorations of seminal works in the humanities and social sciences – books and papers that have had a significant and widely recognised impact on their disciplines. It has been created to serve as much more than just a summary of what lies between the covers of a great book. It illuminates and explores the influences on, ideas of, and impact of that book. Our goal is to offer a learning resource that encourages critical thinking and fosters a better, deeper understanding of important ideas.

Each publication is divided into three Sections: Influences, Ideas, and Impact. Each Section has four Modules. These explore every important facet of the work, and the responses to it.

This Section-Module structure makes a Macat Library book easy to use, but it has another important feature. Because each Macat book is written to the same format, it is possible (and encouraged!) to cross-reference multiple Macat books along the same lines of inquiry or research. This allows the reader to open up interesting interdisciplinary pathways.

To further aid your reading, lists of glossary terms and people mentioned are included at the end of this book (these are indicated by an asterisk [*] throughout) – as well as a list of works cited.

Macat has worked with the University of Cambridge to identify the elements of critical thinking and understand the ways in which six different skills combine to enable effective thinking.
Three allow us to fully understand a problem; three more give us the tools to solve it. Together, these six skills make up the **PACIER** model of critical thinking. They are:

ANALYSIS – understanding how an argument is built
EVALUATION – exploring the strengths and weaknesses of an argument
INTERPRETATION – understanding issues of meaning

CREATIVE THINKING – coming up with new ideas and fresh connections
PROBLEM-SOLVING – producing strong solutions
REASONING – creating strong arguments

To find out more, visit **WWW.MACAT.COM.**

CRITICAL THINKING AND *THE REPUBLIC*

Primary critical thinking skill: ANALYSIS
Secondary critical thinking skill: REASONING

The Republic is Plato's most complete and incisive work – a detailed study of the problem of how best to ensure that justice exists in a real society, rather than as merely the product of an idealized philosophical construct.

The work considers several competing definitions of justice, and looks closely not only at what exactly a "just life" should be, but also at the ways in which society can organise itself in ways that maximize the opportunities for every member to live justly. Much of the discussion is via imagined dialogues, giving Plato the opportunity to deploy the tools of Socratic debate to remarkable effect; nowhere else, it can be argued, is the Socratic dialectic better exemplified than in *The Republic*.

In large measure, Plato's success is the product of the acute analytical ability that he demonstrates throughout his surviving oeuvre. No one is better at understanding the relationships between the various parts of a successful argument than Plato, and *The Republic* also demonstrates the Greek philosopher has few peers when it comes to looking for and highlighting the core assumptions that underlie an argument. The demolition of competing views that Plato puts into the mouth of Socrates is based on a series of relentless interventions and counter-examples that this mastery makes possible.

Combining analytical skills with great powers of reasoning to produce a well-structured solution that deals emphatically with counter-arguments, Plato crafts one of the most enduring works of philosophy in the entire western canon.

ABOUT THE AUTHOR OF THE ORIGINAL WORK

Plato was born in Athens—then the intellectual centre of the ancient world—around 429 BCE. Regarded as the most influential philosopher in the Western tradition of political philosophy, metaphysics, and ethics, Plato was a follower of Socrates and teacher of Aristotle. The founder of the famous Academy—an important center of learning just outside Athens—Plato died around 347 BCE.

ABOUT THE AUTHOR OF THE ANALYSIS

Dr James Orr holds a DPhil in the philosophy of religion from the University of Cambridge. He is currently the McDonald Postdoctoral Fellow in Theology, Ethics, and Public Life at Christ Church College, Oxford.

ABOUT MACAT

GREAT WORKS FOR CRITICAL THINKING

Macat is focused on making the ideas of the world's great thinkers accessible and comprehensible to everybody, everywhere, in ways that promote the development of enhanced critical thinking skills.

It works with leading academics from the world's top universities to produce new analyses that focus on the ideas and the impact of the most influential works ever written across a wide variety of academic disciplines. Each of the works that sit at the heart of its growing library is an enduring example of great thinking. But by setting them in context – and looking at the influences that shaped their authors, as well as the responses they provoked – Macat encourages readers to look at these classics and game-changers with fresh eyes. Readers learn to think, engage and challenge their ideas, rather than simply accepting them.

'Macat offers an amazing first-of-its-kind tool for interdisciplinary learning and research. Its focus on works that transformed their disciplines and its rigorous approach, drawing on the world's leading experts and educational institutions, opens up a world-class education to anyone.'

Andreas Schleicher
Director for Education and Skills, Organisation for Economic
Co-operation and Development

'Macat is taking on some of the major challenges in university education … They have drawn together a strong team of active academics who are producing teaching materials that are novel in the breadth of their approach.'

Prof Lord Broers,
former Vice-Chancellor of the University of Cambridge

'The Macat vision is exceptionally exciting. It focuses upon new modes of learning which analyse and explain seminal texts which have profoundly influenced world thinking and so social and economic development. It promotes the kind of critical thinking which is essential for any society and economy. This is the learning of the future.'

Rt Hon Charles Clarke, former UK Secretary of State for Education

'The Macat analyses provide immediate access to the critical conversation surrounding the books that have shaped their respective discipline, which will make them an invaluable resource to all of those, students and teachers, working in the field.'

Professor William Tronzo, University of California at San Diego

WAYS IN TO THE TEXT

KEY POINTS

- Plato, a philosopher from the Greek city of Athens, lived between 429 and 347 B.C.E.

- His *The Republic* focuses on the simple question of whether it is better to be just or unjust. In addressing this topic, he examines an extraordinary range of questions in ethics, politics, and metaphysics* (the branch of philosophy dealing with fundamental questions about the nature of existence such as time, knowledge, being, and so on).

- Written in the form of a dialogue, *The Republic* is considered by many to be Plato's most important text; it is the first time a Western thinker attempts to set out a comprehensive political vision of a just society.

Who Was Plato?

Plato, the author of *The Republic* (circa 380 B.C.E.), was born around 429 B.C.E. to a wealthy and aristocratic family in Athens at the height of a great artistic and intellectual golden age in the history of the Western tradition.

Athens witnessed enormous turmoil during the fifth century B.C.E. In the first half of the century it successfully defended itself against two foreign invasions from the Persian Empire, the dominant geopolitical force in Asia Minor from the mid-sixth to the mid-fourth

9

century. But by the end of the century it had buckled under the weight of domestic political disasters and war against other Greek states. In some ways, the problems faced by the *polis** (city-state) were the fires that forged the first-ever recognizably democratic form of political arrangement, but the radical nature of its democratically made decisions contributed to its collapse. Athens fell in 404 B.C.E., exhausted by its wars against Sparta* and its allies.

Plato is the author of around 35 philosophical dialogues (a literary form in which a subject is explored as a "discussion" between the author's characters) written in the first half of the fourth century. In 387 B.C.E. he founded the Academy,* an intellectual community named after a sacred grove in Athens dedicated to the local god, Academus. This was an institution that had a deep and extensive influence over Greek and Roman thought for almost nine centuries until it came to an end in 529 C.E. The works produced by people who attended the Academy have had a profound impact on the development of Western thinking.

What Does *The Republic* Say?

The Republic is a dialogue that takes place over the course of 10 books, mainly trying to define justice. It aims to explain the true nature of justice in both the individual and the city-state.

In the aftermath of Athens's rapid political decline at the start of the fourth century, Plato used several dialogues—notably *Laws* and *Statesman*—to unfold a startlingly original vision of the ideal political community. But in *The Republic* his vision is set out more comprehensively and systematically than in any other of his writings. It is difficult to identify another work in the history of ancient political philosophy that encompasses such a dazzling array of issues—issues that move well beyond the traditional confines of the genre itself. *The Republic* is not only a foundational text in political philosophy, but has also shaped a vast range of debates in other branches of philosophy.

Plato's main concern in *The Republic* can be stated simply: what does it mean for individuals and political communities to pursue justice? The text consists of conversations between central characters who discuss the merits of the ethical attitudes that are implicitly endorsed by the Athenian intellectual and political elite of the day.

In book 1, for example, the teacher Thrasymachus* argues that justice is only concerned with satisfying the interests of the powerful ("might-is-right"* or *Machtpolitik**). In book 2, the politician Cleitophon* argues that justice is whatever any individual or group decides it is, regardless of disagreement—an example of ethical relativism* (according to which there are no absolutes in ethical matters, since everything depends on context). This position follows the teaching of the many influential paid traveling teachers of rhetoric* known as Sophists* (from which the English words "sophistry" and "sophistic" are derived to describe clever but empty reasoning).

Plato employs the fictional persona of his teacher Socrates,* one of the most important intellectual figures of ancient Athens, to demonstrate how these commonly held views collapse in the face of relentless interventions and counterexamples. This is the kind of tough examination that we find applied to other concepts in Plato's earlier dialogues: to courage in *Laches*, to piety (or devoutness) in *Euthyphro*, and to wisdom in *Charmides*. Nowhere is the famous "Socratic dialectic"*—which uses group debate to criticize, illuminate, and refine ideas—better exemplified than in *The Republic*.

What distinguishes this dialogue from other dialogues in Plato's work is the extent to which he develops a complex vision of the just individual and society. Not only does *The Republic* discredit existing concepts of justice that do not stand up to critical analysis, it creates new alternatives. Many scholars agree that it is Plato's own views that inform these alternatives, and the method by which it is reached owes much to Socrates.

There are two fundamental questions that underpin this exploration of the nature of justice:

- What does a just life look like and why would it be beneficial to the individual who lived it?
- How can a society organize itself in a way that maximizes opportunities for every individual to live that life?

The key to understanding the connection between these two questions lies in Plato's theory that the nature of the soul and the nature of the city-state exist in relationship to one another. According to this theory, the soul has a structure in three parts—reason, spirit, and desire—and these elements should be reflected in the three-part structure of the city-state: government, protection, and provision. The justice of both soul and city-state is achieved by finding a balance between the three elements.

Why Does *The Republic* Matter?

The breadth and sophistication of the discussions in *The Republic* are unlike any philosophical examinations of the machinery of the political community that came before. The work's characters chisel away at issues that are still part of important cultural and political debates in the twenty-first century, such as:

- the rule of law
- whether propaganda should be allowed
- the status of human rights—what Plato calls "moral claims"
- the danger of representing reality in creative expression and that doing so may create an illusory world that could lead someone away from the real (Plato would almost certainly have included broadcast and digital media in this category)
- the question of how gender relates to the allocation of social roles
- the problems of distinguishing knowledge (moral or otherwise) from belief and mere opinion
- education theory and its importance to the development of a flourishing society.

Before *The Republic*, no work existed that addressed universal problems like these in the context of a developing city-state. In other words, the text is more important than any other to the discipline of political philosophy. Without it, it is almost impossible to understand the structure of political thought that followed. Its influence, however, is not confined to what it has contributed to political philosophy. The text broaches many questions in the areas of metaphysics (the philosophical study of the fundamental ingredients of reality), epistemology* (the philosophical study of knowledge and belief), aesthetics* (the philosophical study of the nature of beauty), and metaethics* (the philosophical study of the fundamental character of goodness and moral obligation). It can also claim to be the first work that attempts to reflect systematically on a society's responsibilities for educating its citizens.

Many of Plato's discussions of these questions continue to play a role in contemporary debates, and no other ancient philosopher except Aristotle can lay claim to such a legacy. Yet even the enormous philosophical contributions of Aristotle would not have been possible were it not for the decades he spent engaging with Plato's dialogues.

SECTION 1
INFLUENCES

MODULE 1
THE AUTHOR AND THE
HISTORICAL CONTEXT

KEY POINTS

- *The Republic* is the product of a turbulent period in the political history of Classical Greece.

- *The Republic* represents the closest we have to a systematic vision of moral and political life in classical philosophy.

- Plato's teacher Socrates* is still important to Western political philosophy, partly as a result of Plato's representation of him in *The Republic*.

Why Read this Text?

Many introductions to Plato's *The Republic* include a comment by Alfred North Whitehead,* co-editor of the classic mathematics text *Principia Mathematica* (1910–13) with the British philosopher Bertrand Russell.* Whitehead says that Western philosophy is "but a series of footnotes to Plato."[1] If that is true, then the most heavily annotated would be his finest work, *The Republic*.

Before looking at the philosophical content of *The Republic*, we should first place Plato in the context of Athens itself. This was a city whose culture reached the greatest heights imaginable, but which eventually degenerated into totalitarianism*—a system of government in which the citizen is utterly subject to the state—after costly bouts of civil war. These years were exceptionally turbulent in the history of Greek civilization. One crucial reason for the text's lasting importance is that it is a work of political philosophy that emerged from a practical understanding of the importance of its subject. The consequences of failing to develop a truly inclusive and ordered political community

> ❝ [Plato] would have been old enough to witness with young and impressionable eyes the last scenes of a tragedy, the decline and fall of the Athenian Empire. ❞
>
> R. M. Hare, *Plato*

had become all too apparent. Given the many catastrophic experiments in applying utopian* but totalitarian ideologies in the twentieth century, the thinking that motivated Plato to write *The Republic* is no less important today than it was in fifth-century B.C.E. Athens. The dialogue is the first in the history of European political thought to try to set out a systematic and comprehensive vision of what a just society looks like, as well as a vision of how citizens might develop the necessary moral character to make it a reality.

Author's Life
Plato was born into a wealthy and well-connected Athenian family towards the end of the Peloponnesian War* between Athens and the allies and forces of Sparta* that dominated the second half of the fifth century B.C.E.[2] In his teenage years, he would have witnessed the consequences of the catastrophic failure of Athens to colonize* the Mediterranean island of Sicily in 415 B.C.E. He would have seen at first hand the dangerous tactics of Greek popular rulers—a particular kind of politician prone to manipulating the fears of the lower classes to seize personal power.

When Plato was in his early twenties, Athens flirted with a moderate oligarchy* (an elite group of rulers) in 411 B.C.E. before the city descended into chaos during the so-called "Rule of the Thirty" period starting in 404 B.C.E. This political catastrophe occurred when the so-called Thirty Tyrants,* aristocratic members of Athenian society chosen by their Spartan victors, seized power in the immediate wake of Athens's total exhaustion in the Peloponnesian War. The oligarchy lasted little more than a year but the destruction it brought about was significant. One in 20 Athenians lost their lives, a great deal of the property of its citizens was seized by the authorities, and many who were considered to be a threat to the Thirty on the basis of their support for democracy were exiled.

At the end of this period of oligarchic oppression, in 399 B.C.E., Plato's teacher Socrates was put on trial for, as Ancient Greek historian Xenophon* records, "introducing new gods" and "corrupting the youth."[3] Plato's shock at the persecution of his master led to a self-imposed exile from Athens, and its collapsing empire across the Mediterranean, to Sicily. Here, he became tutor to the son of Dionysius I of Syracuse,* the tyrant of the island. It was, in all likelihood, a pointed rejection of the chaos that a nakedly populist democracy had unleashed in Athens, and one which was more and more in line with Plato's distinctly anti-democratic political vision.

Author's Background

This time of great political unrest is the crucial historical backdrop against which Plato's body of work unfolds, and against which we must try to interpret *The Republic* in particular. Considering the historical context, it is less surprising that the greed, aggression, and spirit of moral compromise that characterized Athens in the second half of the fifth century prompted so many intellectuals—and Plato in particular—to doubt that democracy was the most satisfactory form of political arrangement.

The criticism of Athenian democracy's vulnerability to demagoguery and popular hysteria can be seen in many of Plato's dialogues. *The Republic*, in particular, includes exchanges with an anti-democratic spirit that is more marked than in any other of his works.[4] Part of what had permitted the manipulation of the Athenian citizenry was a widespread and unscrupulous use of the arts of rhetoric* promoted by the traveling philosophy teachers known as the Sophists*—the majority of whom were not citizens themselves.

Another important element in Plato's background is the time he spent in Sicily as the guest of Dionysius I, the cruel and dictatorial ruler of Syracuse, a city Athens had unsuccessfully attempted to attack in 415 B.C.E. Plato's visits to Sicily seem to have been triggered by his deep discontent with the trial of Socrates that ended with his execution at the hands of the Thirty Tyrants in 399 B.C.E.

NOTES

1   Alfred North Whitehead, *Process and Reality*, part II (Cambridge: Cambridge University Press, 1929), chapter 3.

2   See Thucydides, *History of the Peloponnesian War*, trans. Rex Warner (New York: Penguin Classics, 1972).

3   Xenophon, *Apology,* trans. O. J. Todd (Harvard, MA: Harvard University Press, 2003), §§10–13.

4   See Simon Hornblower, "Greece: The History of the Classical Period," in *The Oxford History of Greece and the Hellenistic World,* John Boardman et al., eds (Oxford: Oxford University Press, 2001), 142–76.

MODULE 2
ACADEMIC CONTEXT

KEY POINTS

- Plato situates the action and conversation of *The Republic* symbolically on the road from Athens to its harbor, the Piraeus, and the home of the wealthy "metic"* (a resident of Athens who did not have full political rights) Cephalus* and his son Polemarchus.*

- Plato uses the characters of his elder brother Glaucon,* the traveling teacher Thrasymachus,* and the politician Cleitophon* to challenge what he sees as failed answers to the question of why people should be just.

- The dialogue opposes the approach to philosophy and education adopted by the traveling teachers known as Sophists,* personified by Thrasymachus.

The Work In Its Context

The Republic gives us a great insight into the extraordinary range of Plato's thought; it is difficult to think of a significant philosophical theme left untouched.

The work opens with Plato's former teacher, the philosopher Socrates,* strolling down to the Piraeus port area—a few miles from Athens—with Plato's brother Glaucon, before being invited into the home of a wealthy businessman, Cephalus, by his son Polemarchus. Given the subject matter of *The Republic*, it may seem odd for Plato to have set the dialogue outside the city. Cephalus is a *metoikos* or "metic": a man not eligible for Athenian citizenship, but who—like Plato's student Aristotle*—migrated to Athens from another city-state to make his living in Piraeus. Piraeus was a natural choice of location for

> ❝ It is on the face of it unlikely that all the ideas we find in his dialogues were newly-minted; and in fact there is quite a lot of evidence that they were not. Originality in philosophy often consists not in having new thoughts, but in making clear what was not clear before. ❞
>
> R. M. Hare, *Plato*

fortune-seeking men like Cephalus as it benefited from being a major port at the height of Athens's expansion following its military struggle with Sparta* and her allies.

Although this setting may seem strange, it's unlikely to have been accidental, given Plato's constant attention to detail throughout his dialogues. The setting is probably intended to be symbolic: the political vision that unfolds is one at odds with the democratic and oligarchic* governments that Athens had known to that point, and this may be reflected in Plato's decision to set the dialogue outside the city itself.

Overview of the Field

The main intellectual context in which we understand *The Republic* is the Sophist movement that existed in fifth-century B.C.E. Greek city-states. The Sophists were teachers, largely itinerant, who taught rhetoric*—the art of persuasive speech—for money. Many of the dialogue-partners in Platonic dialogues are historical Sophists.

One of the most aggressive representatives of the Sophist tradition was Thrasymachus of Chalcedon. For Plato, the Sophists had corrupted what he considered to be the sacred search for truth. They were known for prizing rhetorical success over philosophical truth, and, even worse, doing so for money. Their students were encouraged to develop a style of debate that prioritized combativeness and point-scoring over the search for real truth. Gorgias,* a pre-Socratic* philosopher, wrote an influential collection entitled *Dissoi Logoi* ("Double-Sayings") which is a perfect example of this style. Although Gorgias does not feature as a character in *The Republic* itself, the antagonism and intellectual pettiness for which he was well known are reflected in the personality of Thrasymachus.

The first book of *The Republic* demonstrates Plato's hostility to the approach that *Dissoi Logoi* encouraged. Philosophical discussion between Socrates and Thrasymachus quickly breaks down, suggesting that the "might-is-right"* view of the latter prevents a real inquiry of truth. His idea that justice should exist to serve the most powerful in society makes politics and philosophy nothing more than a trial of strength. The brutal *realpolitik*—the exercise of power without regard to morality or ideology—that led to the decline of Athens in the final decades of the fifth century can be attributed to this approach.

Academic Influences

By far the most important influence on Plato was his teacher Socrates, who introduced a way of thinking that differed so much from any previous approach that historians now label the philosophical figures that came before him as "pre-Socratic." The work of these thinkers forms at least some of the intellectual background from which *The Republic* emerged. Although their work only survives in fragmentary form, we know that many of these philosophers—most notably Thales,* Anaximander,* Anaximenes,* and Heraclitus*—tried to understand the physical world in terms of a single substance (such as water, air, or fire). For that reason, they have sometimes been described as the world's first natural scientists.

This sort of exercise is very different from any that Plato undertakes in *The Republic*, but bearing the pre-Socratics in mind helps us to understand one philosophical quest that guides much of *The Republic*:

Plato tries to uncover the ultimate constituents of reality. His answer departed from those of his pre-Socratic predecessors dramatically. He claimed that the physical world was less real than the world in which Forms* (things that cannot be sensed but that are, according to Plato, more real than things that *can* be sensed) were located, amounting to a rejection of their entire project.

MODULE 3
THE PROBLEM

KEY POINTS

- The central problem of *The Republic* is the nature of justice and its relationship to individuals, specifically as citizens of a just political community.

- A related difficulty to the central problem is how we know what objective goodness is (the "Form of the Good") and how best to achieve this knowledge.

- Established theories about the nature of justice (that it consists either in meeting the demands of the stronger party, or by conforming to social arrangements that a community has reached) are considered as a means to construct a viable alternative.

Core Question

Plato's *The Republic* opens with a simple problem: what is justice (*dikaiosune*)? And is the person who acts justly happier than the person who does not?

Plato uses these two focal points to explore a huge variety of philosophical issues. Some of the discussions that stem from the central problem concern the following:

- the role of women in the ideal city-state
- the fundamental character of ultimate reality
- the psychology of happiness and the way happiness relates to individual morality
- pedagogy* (theories about the best ways of educating)
- the nature of philosophical exchange
- the challenges of *realpolitik**
- the nature of the soul

❝ So now the whole conversation has left me in the dark; for so long as I do not know what justice is, I am hardly likely to know whether or not it is a virtue, or whether it makes a man happy or unhappy. ❞

Socrates, *The Republic* 354

- the nature of goodness
- the problem of universals*
- the structure of a radically communitarian* society (a society that emphasizes the individual's role in the community)
- different theories of state and civic life, and how to lead a worthwhile life within those structures.

Beneath the central problem of defining justice lies an essential question: how can knowledge of the good be attained? This is a question that Plato's "Allegory* of the Cave" intends to address. It leads him to then ask what a city-state should do to equip its citizens to recognize and pursue the good.

The Participants

Cephalus* and Thrasymachus* base their conception of justice on a belief that human beings interact with each other in selfish and competitive ways. This approach reaches a conspicuous impasse. Plato wants his readers to understand that in the hands of Thrasymachus, the Sophistic* method—consisting of confusing rhetoric,* aggressive posturing, ethical relativism,* contradictory conclusions—will hinder rather than help the pursuit of truth. We should not ignore the fact that after the end of book 1, Thrasymachus does not make any further contribution to *The Republic*. His silence represents Plato's decision to sideline Sophistic approaches early on, before the development of his constructive project: Socrates'* account of the ideal city-state in books 2, 3, and 4.

The second phase of discussion, led by Plato's brothers Glaucon* and Adeimantus* in book 2, offers an alternative solution to the central problem identified earlier. It analyzes what contemporary political theory would label a contractarian* definition of justice—the idea that justice is not the satisfaction of the stronger party's desires, but is obedience to laws agreed upon by consensus within a community. An important factor motivating many contractarian theories is a degree of pessimism about human nature. In its boldest form, as we find it in the work of the influential British political philosopher Thomas Hobbes,* contractarianism is built on a profound cynicism about the behavior of human beings in a "state of nature."[1] The thinking is that the more pessimistic people are about human behavior, the more likely they are to insist on agreements between citizens to keep the darker side of human nature in check.

These are the two backdrops against which a radically new vision of justice unfolds, as well as the political structure necessary to realize it. It is crucial to note that both failed approaches—the "might-is-right"* philosophy of Thrasymachus and Cleitophon,* and the contractarianism of Glaucon and Adeimantus—are relativistic positions. From both perspectives, justice is understood as relative to the superior strength of a given party, or relative to the cultural preferences a particular community commits to law.

The Contemporary Debate

Plato's aim is to demonstrate the dangerous implications of the Sophistic position, before offering an alternative. An extended idea is laid out of what a well-ordered society should look like, and how it should reflect the threefold structure of Plato's theory of the soul. Following the critiques of the *Machtpolitik** of Thrasymachus in book I (the politics of "might-is-right"), the relativism of Cleitophon at the beginning of book 2, and the contractarianism of Glaucon, some of *The Republic*'s central constructive arguments begin to unfold.

The Republic's main concern is how to live justly. The proposed solution is a form of social, cultural, and political organization that mirrors human psychology in the primitive terms that Plato understood it. This ideal state would accommodate a variety of specialization among its citizens. The principle that each individual has a specific role to which he or she is best suited determines the organizational logic of Socrates' ideal city-state.

The first two books of *The Republic* set up the problem that will motivate the constructive vision explored in the subsequent eight.

NOTES

1   See Lesley Brown, "Glaucon's Challenge, Rational Egoism and Ordinary Morality," in *Pursuing the Good: Ethics and Metaphysics in Plato's Republic,* Douglas Cairns et al., eds (Edinburgh: Edinburgh University Press, 2007), 42–60.

MODULE 4
THE AUTHOR'S CONTRIBUTION

KEY POINTS

- *The Republic* left a more enduring legacy for Western political thought than any other of Plato's works or, arguably, any other ancient work of philosophy.

- *The Republic* is the first text to think about the organization of political communities in a methodical way, and the first to make a connection between the nature of a community and the nature of the individuals within it.

- The dialogue has had an impact on almost every chapter in the history of European intellectual thought.

Author's Aims

One of Plato's aims in *The Republic* is to conduct philosophical inquiry in a style that differed from the philosophical writings that had preceded it. The form of dialogue itself, in which almost his entire body of work is composed, has had some notable examples in the history of philosophy: the Roman philosopher Cicero's* *On the Nature of the Gods* (54–51 B.C.E.), the medieval thinker Boethius's* *De Consolatione Philosophiae* (composed around 525 C.E.), the British philosopher George Berkeley's* *Three Dialogues* (1713), and the Scottish philosopher David Hume's* *Dialogues on Natural Religion* (1779). But *The Republic* was not just a stylistic departure. It was also remarkable for its sense of moral urgency, an attitude that contrasted sharply with that of the Sophists* (the traveling teachers of rhetoric* who taught for money). It was this that distinguished Plato's influence from so much subsequent philosophy in the Western tradition.

The most important of Plato's aims in *The Republic* is not to showcase the most appropriate way to convey philosophical ideas, but

> 66 The safest general characterization of the European philosophical tradition is that it consists of a series of footnotes to Plato. 99
>
> Alfred North Whitehead, *Process and Reality*

to make a successful case for the ideas themselves. Although he had explored some of these in earlier dialogues, *The Republic* reveals the scope of his thought more fully than any other work.

Approach

The main idea of the dialogue can be broken down into two distinct but related parts. In the first part, Plato's teacher Socrates* claims that the chief characteristic of the just society is that it encourages its citizens to understand justice for themselves.[1] The just society ensures that every citizen is assigned a function appropriate to their abilities.[2] He says that each political community has three principal functions: to ensure that it is governed properly,[3] that it is adequately protected,[4] and that it is able to sustain itself in material terms.[5] The task of a society is to allocate citizens to each of these three functions in a way that matches their skills: those with the most intelligence should rule it, the strongest should protect it, and those with the greatest artistic and technical abilities should provide for it.[6]

The second part relates to the souls of individual citizens, which should mirror the tiered organization of the just society. To Socrates, individual morality does not consist in the self-interest of the strong (as the Sophist Thrasymachus* proposes) nor in arbitrary social conventions (as Plato's brother Glaucon* suggests), but rather in developing a soul that successfully balances its three elements—its rational, spirited, and appetitive dimensions. The soul has the same three functions as a political community, namely to govern, protect, and sustain itself. The just soul, like the just society, allocates the appropriate elements to their relevant functions. The purpose of the soul is to govern the individual citizen, the purpose of the spirit is to protect it, and the purpose of the appetitive is to supply its material needs.[7] The soul that fulfills all three of these purposes is a just one.

Contribution in Context

There are many other important ideas in *The Republic*, but the discussions of this twofold idea—the nature of the just society and the nature of the just person—represent Plato's most original contribution to Western thought. The idea brings into view some significant questions that still engage contemporary thinkers (the nature and role of citizens within a society, for example).[8]

Apart from its specific contribution to Western philosophy, one of *The Republic*'s most important achievements is that it encourages its readers to reflect on what makes societies just, and on the connection between a just society and the moral conduct of its citizens. No philosopher had previously attempted such a comprehensive vision of political life, and very few of the political philosophers who attempted to do so after Plato—from his student Aristotle* in the fourth century B.C.E. to the diplomat and political theorist Niccolò Machiavelli* in the sixteenth century, and including influential political theorists from Leo Strauss* to John Rawls* in the twentieth century—have not been influenced in some way by his contribution to political thought.

NOTES

1   Plato, *The Republic*, trans. Robin Waterfield (Oxford: Oxford University Press, 1993), 592a–b.

2   Plato, *The Republic*, 435b.

3   Plato, *The Republic*, 369b.

4   Plato, *The Republic*, 374.

5   Plato, *The Republic,* 428d.

6   Plato, *The Republic*, 434.

7   Plato, *The Republic*, 441e.

8   For debate over Plato's definition of justice, see David Sachs, "A Fallacy in Plato's *Republic*," *Philosophical Review* 72, no. 2 (1963): 141–58; and Richard Kraut, "The Defense of Justice in Plato's *Republic*," in *Plato's Republic: Critical Essays,* ed. Richard Kraut (New York: Rowman and Littlefield, 1997), 1–16.

SECTION 2
IDEAS

MODULE 5
MAIN IDEAS

KEY POINTS

- The first idea of *The Republic* is that justice and self-interest coexist in an individual's life.

- The second idea is that justice for an individual—which is the possession of a well-ordered soul—is also what underpins the just society.

- A third important question is the challenge of devising a political community that is itself just, and allows justice to prosper among its citizens.

Key Themes

The main focus of Plato's *The Republic* is the definition of social justice and individual morality. Plato opens up three main responses to this task, each of which raises the questions of what it is to be a just society, and what it is to be a just participant in society. Although they are distinct problems, they are also connected, since Plato—like his student, the philosopher Aristotle*—generally takes it for granted that human beings are intrinsically social and political beings.

First, Plato considers the position that "justice" is whatever the most powerful individuals say it is—the argument made by the Athenian generals in the section of the ancient historian Thucydides'* *History of the Peloponnesian War* known as the "Melian Dialogue."[1] In his *The Republic*, Plato gives this argument to the character of Thrasymachus.*

Second, Plato considers the argument that a just government requires citizens of all stations to observe the social conventions that

66 Thus we know that *the Republic* is centrally about justice and our good, and about the knowledge of the good required for understanding and bringing justice, happiness, and good government into our lives and our societies. **99**

Gerasimos Santas, *Understanding Plato's Republic*

make possible a consensus between those who are governed and those who govern. The characters given the names of his brothers Glaucon* and Adeimantus* put forward this point of view.

Third, Plato considers the possibility that an objective reality exists independently of human power and human agreement. Crucially, Plato argues that a life that makes justice its principle aim is one most oriented towards happiness and fulfillment—happiness and fulfillment meaning an individual who has developed a balanced soul (specifically, a proper ordering of the reasoning, spirited, and appetitive aspects of the soul).

Exploring the Ideas

The central idea of *The Republic* is that the third approach is the most convincing answer to the problem. It envisages a moral world that exists independently of the interests of individual citizens and independently of anything that a society agrees upon. The physical world represents an imperfect reflection of a more substantial reality, towards which philosophers must guide their pupils (or, in the case of philosopher-rulers, their citizens). Gaining knowledge of this objective goodness is achieved through education, specifically education by means of the Socratic* method, in which a particular problem is subjected to *elenchus**: examination conducted through the asking of questions. As a result, *The Republic* returns again and again to questions of education and how best to achieve it; the dialogue contains elaborate analogies and thought experiments, most famously those of "Gyges' Ring,"[2] the "Analogy of the Sun,"[3] the "Analogy of the Divided Line,"[4] the "City-Soul Analogy,"*[5] and the "Allegory* of the Cave."[6]

One of the most controversial ideas in *The Republic* is a profound suspicion of the democratic process. This suspicion motivates Socrates' proposal that the ideal city-state consists of a hierarchy, with executive power resting in the hands of the philosopher-rulers. The application of this principle is fundamentally anti-democratic, as illustrated by the ship-of-state analogy.[7] Socrates describes a ship-owner (representing the people) who is physically frail and unfamiliar with navigating ships, so that his sailors (the populist politicians or demagogues) vie with one another to command his vessel in order to steal its goods. A captain is required to steer the ship-of-state who has adequate knowledge of navigation (astronomy, meteorology, and so on)—in other words, the guardian*-rulers who have devoted themselves to pursuing the Form of the Good. The argument increases in intensity in book 8 of *The Republic*, which makes the case that democracy will always be vulnerable to the whims of a fickle public and the ambitions of charismatic populists, and is therefore inherently unstable.

In this vision of society, the reasoning aspect of the soul is represented by the philosopher-rulers, the spirited component is represented by their subordinates, and the appetitive component is represented by the workers. Just as the three parts of the soul are interdependent and operate harmoniously within the soul of the just *person*, it is a mark of the just *society* that it integrates all three of its fundamental constituents in a balanced way. The exchanges in *The Republic* return repeatedly to this idea; much of the political vision described rests on a recurring analogy between the three-part structure of the human body and the equivalent structure of the city-state.

Language and Expression

Like all of Plato's texts, the dialogue is written as a conversation, which gives a lightness and momentum to the complex journey on which he takes us. Plato was a great advocate of Attic Greek, the language in which the original text was written, and no translation can fully capture the elegance of the original, though some translators have come close. Many of the virtues of Plato's language are impossible to convey to those with no knowledge of the original Greek, particularly in light of the way that the text is enriched by the use of particles: small words, adverbs and conjunctives, that modulate the sense and nuance of sentences in subtle ways. Perhaps only the eighteenth-century Scottish philosopher David Hume* in his *Dialogues Concerning Natural Religion* comes close to emulating the sense of effortlessness and grace that characterizes Plato's style in *The Republic*.

In *The Republic* we find far more sophisticated monologues than conversational exchanges, principally made by Socrates but also other contributors such as Glaucon and Adeimantus. This is with the exception of the opening book, which in many ways resembles the language and expression of Plato's earlier dialogues, among them *Euthyphro* and *Lysis*.

NOTES

1   Thucydides, *History of the Peloponnesian War*, trans. Rex Warner (New York: Penguin Classics, 1972), 5.86–116.

2   Plato, The Republic, trans. Robin Waterfield (Oxford: Oxford University Press, 1993), 359a–360d.

3   Plato, *The Republic*, 514a–520a.

4   Plato, *The Republic*, 509d–511e.

5   Plato, *The Republic*, 368c–369a.

6   Plato, *The Republic*, 507b–509c.

7   Plato, *The Republic*, 488c.

MODULE 6
SECONDARY IDEAS

KEY POINTS

- Many of the secondary ideas in *The Republic* are advanced through the use of "myths" or "analogies."

- Plato gives philosophers a central role in the governance of the city-state, so the question of how best to educate them is significant in *The Republic*.

- Plato's insistence that poets and artists should be excluded from the political community has attracted criticism in the last century.

Other Ideas

The secondary ideas of Plato's *The Republic* include reflections on the equal distribution of roles between the sexes, the contribution of education to society, and the extent to which a society should exert control over the artistic expression of its citizens.

One of the most remarkable features of Plato's *The Republic* is Socrates'* extended arguments that women should be treated with complete equality as prospective citizens in the ideal *polis** (city-state).

Education and its relationship to the just city-state is a theme combined with almost all others in *The Republic*. Socrates' vision puts the philosophical formation of its citizens at the heart of constitutional logic. The task of education is to generate and preserve civic loyalty to the *polis*. A universal education system is proposed in which every citizen is educated until the age of 18. Those who work in a productive capacity—farmers, workers, craftsmen—would finish their education at that point and begin work. Those with particular talent would be educated further. The latter group comprises the social group who

" Plato discusses many subjects in *the Republic*: the uses and misuses of wealth, competing theories of what justice is, rival conceptions of human happiness, the relation of justice to happiness, early and advanced education, religion and theology, private property, the other virtues of cities and of individuals, the human soul and human motivations. **"**

Gerasimos Santas, *Understanding Plato's Republic*

would perform military and police service for the defense and stability of the city.[1] A second group of gifted citizens would receive philosophical training for several more years to prepare for their roles as philosopher-rulers.[2]

A notable feature of civic education set out in *The Republic* is the exclusion of any kind of poetry or art that does not emphasize the virtues of service to the city-state.

Exploring the Ideas

Given the overwhelmingly masculine concerns of the political, social, and intellectual life of fifth-century Athens, these proposals were revolutionary. Athenian women were—as a legal matter—possessions to be bequeathed to others, in the same as any other belonging. Courtesans (*hetairai**) were a notable feature of the city at that time.[3]

Books 2 and 3 of *The Republic* include exchanges that were overtly hostile towards poets and artists. The main criticism was that they appealed to the baser emotions (philosophers would call these "affections") rather than to rational principles. This view is more plausibly attributed to Plato himself than to the historical Socrates. Book 2 ends by questioning the role of poetry and art in the perfect city-state. The conclusion reached is that they are permissible only when they can be used to educate the prospective "guardians"* of the *polis*.

Proposals for a limited form of censorship in this early stage of the work are brought up again towards the end of book 10, which focuses more on the psychological responses of a student engaging with complex poetry or art. In the course of these discussions, the "Allegory of the Divided Line" is introduced. This thought experiment invites us to think of reality as a line that places entities in order, according to their degree of reality. This allegory* is one of Plato's tools to persuade us to understand reality as two domains: the domain of the mind, and the domain of matter. This particular form of dualism* would have a far-reaching influence in the history of Western thought.

The fundamental objection leveled at poetry and the arts (here Plato includes Homer, the Greek lyric poets, and the work of the great Athenian tragedians) is that these media are representational. Such works of art present a version of reality intrinsically distorted by the artist and the genre into which it falls. In other words, the arts are structurally deceptive—the failure to present reality in an unmediated way is inherent in the aims of an artist.

From our current perspective, this objection to artistic freedom seems odd. The argument that artists should contribute to the success of a political community has had a measurable impact we can still see today. It's more striking than ever in the wake of a century that saw more widespread use of propaganda as a tool of political oppression than any other.

Overlooked

The Republic has been examined more carefully than almost any other text in the Western tradition and there are almost no angles that have been left unexplored. Its various interpretations are intrinsically shaped by the political circumstances from which they have developed. At the midpoint of the twentieth century much debate turned on the problem of whether Plato's vision of an ideal society was overly authoritarian* (that is, whether the governmental principles it proposes function at the expense of the liberty of the citizen). In practical terms, it could be argued that the dialogue's central thesis influenced the utopian* politics that marked the twentieth century—notably Soviet communism. Different themes and topics may well assume an importance for future generations that we cannot currently predict. It is the mark of a great philosophical text that it continues to provide new insight into a society's intellectual and cultural life, and there is no reason for thinking that *The Republic* will not achieve this in the future.

NOTES

1   Plato, *The Republic*, trans. Robin Waterfield (Oxford: Oxford University Press, 1993), 436.

2   Plato, *The Republic,* 442a.

3   On the fascinating world of the Athenian *demi-monde* in this period, see James Davidson's *Courtesans and Fishcakes: Consuming Passions in Classical Athens* (London: HarperCollins, 1997).

MODULE 7
ACHIEVEMENT

KEY POINTS

- The achievements of Plato's dialogue are its influence on subsequent thought, both through the method it uses to convey its ideas and through the power of the ideas themselves.

- The dialogue gave Western thought a means of evaluating and comparing competing visions of individual morality and social justice.

- *The Republic* also opened up a vast range of philosophical questions that continue to occupy modern thinkers.

Assessing The Argument

The scale of Plato's enduring achievement in *The Republic* is enormous. It was the first serious philosophical reflection on the nature of political justice and individual morality. It is also the first example in Western thought of a systematic attempt to define the nature of fundamental reality, concentrating particularly on the nature of goodness and how we can come to know it. Plato's account of the soul is the first suggestion that we seek justice for the sake of pursuing objective goodness, and not just for reasons of individual self-interest.

Leaving these achievements aside, the central claim that social justice and individual morality should be understood in terms of balance and order has not been widely agreed. After all, it seems perfectly possible for societies and individuals to achieve the balance Plato promotes and still practice injustice and immorality. Justice and morality are not intrinsic features of the proportionate distribution of a state's functions or a person's faculties. This is the concern that has occupied the most perceptive critics of *The Republic* in recent decades.

❝ [*The Republic*] is undoubtedly the grandest of all [Plato's] compositions; including in itself all his different points of excellence. **❞**
George Grote, *Plato and Other Companions of Sokrates*

Since Plato fails to connect his definition of the just soul with practically applied good behavior, it seems that Socrates* is left with no convincing answer to those who would follow the characters Thrasymachus* and Cleitophon*—for whom justice is a matter of aggression successfully executed.

According to the logic of *The Republic*, it would be possible to advocate aggression and violence and still maintain that one's soul was just. Nothing in what Socrates says about the nature of individual morality rejects this contradiction.

Achievement in Context

Plato's achievement is more than just a contribution to political philosophy—it made all subsequent political philosophy possible. His recurrent interest in the themes of justice and fairness also characterizes some of the most important recent figures in political philosophy, among them the influential liberal* thinker John Rawls,*[1] the American libertarian* philosopher Robert Nozick,*[2] the communitarian* philosopher Michael Sandel,*[3] and the Indian scholar Amartya Sen.*[4] Only certain of Plato's student Aristotle's* very best works—such as *Metaphysics*, *Politics*, and *Nicomachean Ethics*—can boast a similar degree of influence on contemporary thinking.

Although Plato's ideas in *The Republic* have by no means been universally accepted, the fact that some of the most vital thinkers of the last century have thought it necessary to criticize them testifies indirectly to their importance. It is partly as a result of this work that schools of philosophers sprung up in the Hellenistic* period (323–31 B.C.E.). Schools such as the Stoics and so-called Academic Skeptics (an

influential group of skeptics named after Plato's school, the Academy)
continued to exercise an important influence right up to the dawn of
the second millennium C.E. through figures such as the third-century
philosophers Plotinus* and Porphyry,* both of whom founded their
thought on that of Plato.

Limitations

Contemporary thinkers—particularly those writing in the tradition of
political liberalism*—are reluctant to construct their philosophy
around the kind of metaphysical* theorizing we see in *The Republic*.
Rawls (at least in his early period) thinks it is better that his account of
justice consists of an "argument that does not rely on any special
metaphysical or philosophical doctrine,"[5] by which he means that his
argument should look to material and worldly causes, proofs, and
analysis. "Metaphysical" in this sense relates to the branch of philosophy
that inquires into the basic principles of existence and the frequently
abstract reasoning with which that inquiry is conducted.

There are two reasons why this need not undermine the
achievement of *The Republic*. First, the vision of the ideal society given
in the dialogue is separable in principle from the metaphysical claims
that accompany it. Second, figures such as Rawls have been repeatedly
criticized—notably by his colleague at Harvard, Michael Sandel—for
assuming that any political account of justice could be formulated in a
vacuum without the influence of metaphysics.

It's arguable that no theory in political philosophy can really be
free of prior assumptions relating to the nature of reality. Is it possible
to realize a convincing theory of justice without an existing notion of
human nature? Or without addressing whether goodness exists
objectively, or as a result of social conditioning? If we are swayed by
these criticisms, then the attempt to divorce metaphysics from political
philosophy is flawed, and the implied criticism of *The Republic*'s aims
needs to be treated with caution.

NOTES

1   John Rawls, *A Theory of Justice* (Harvard, MA: Harvard University Press, 1971).

2   Robert Nozick, *Anarchy, State, and Utopia* (New York: Basic Books, 1974).

3   Michael J. Sandel, *Liberalism and the Limits of Justice* (Cambridge: Cambridge University Press, 1982).

4   Amartya Sen, *The Idea of Justice* (Harvard, MA: Harvard University Press, 2009).

5   Rawls, *Theory of Justice*, 188.

MODULE 8
PLACE IN THE AUTHOR'S LIFE AND WORK

KEY POINTS

- The precise position of *The Republic* in the timeline of Plato's 35 dialogues is heavily contested.

- The traditional cataloging of Plato's body of work identifies the dialogue as a product of the so-called Middle period.

- According to some recent scholarship, however, the methods used to determine the order and dating of Plato's dialogues have been inaccurate and cannot be relied on.

Positioning

It's difficult to establish the precise sequence in which Plato composed his dialogues. The most concrete piece of evidence we have is Aristotle's* claim that his teacher wrote *The Republic* before he wrote his *Laws*.[1] Technical analysis of stylistic aspects of Plato's dialogues has revealed a number of interesting possibilities.[2] This approach—known as stylometry—involves tracking the frequency and distribution of particular words, phrases, and grammatical quirks throughout an author's body of work.

There are, of course, legitimate concerns regarding whether it is possible to reach conclusions about authorship and the timeframe of a particular work on this basis; it is at best an inexact science. For example, we know that it was fairly common practice for established thinkers to dictate their work to scribes, which may account for many of the stylistic differences. Nevertheless, for the most part it is clear that these conclusions are consistent with the previously established chronology; stylometric analysis, in other words, confirms analyses carried out independently of stylometry.

❝ *The Republic* is especially interesting in this connection because it is overtly transitional. Book I has the form of a Socratic dialogue like the early ones; but the rest of the book is a continuous exposition of what we can only take to be Plato's own views on people and society. **❞**

Julia Annas, *An Introduction to Plato's Republic*

Integration

Despite these difficulties, it is generally agreed that *The Republic* was written after Plato's Early period—when he produced dialogues whose ideas are thought to capture those of his teacher Socrates most accurately—and towards the end of the Middle period, shortly before the other two great works of the Late period, *Protagoras* and *Theatetus*. The Middle period is generally considered to begin with the founding of his school, the Academy,* in 387 B.C.E. and to continue until 367 B.C.E., the date of his second visit to Sicily to tutor the son of the tyrant Dionysius I of Syracuse.*

When considering the development of Plato's political thought, *The Republic* can be viewed as the first in a trilogy alongside two other dialogues that focus principally on political questions: *Statesman* and *Laws*.

In *Statesman*, Plato argued that to successfully run a city-state for the benefit of its citizens requires a specialized form of knowledge (*gnosis*). This position is a natural development from the focus on pedagogy* and philosophical education that we find in *The Republic*. By contrast, *Laws* sets out a second utopian* vision, but one that appears to be more "Platonic" than "Socratic." The dialogue offers a complex description of an idealized community based on the fictional island of Magnesia. Although the relationship between *The Republic* and *Laws* is the subject of much debate, it seems likely that Plato came to realize that the limits of human nature and rationality made the ideal city-state an unattainable dream. What was required, as the next best alternative, was a state whose citizens were separated into three divisions and extensively trained in philosophy with limited access to art.

Significance

The difficulty in precisely situating *The Republic* in the development of Plato's thought should not obscure the widespread agreement among scholars that its ideas represent Plato's own position in a unique way. Some of the shorter and less philosophically complex dialogues seem to reflect the concerns of the historical Socrates more so than Plato's own.

The dialogue is now commonly considered to be Plato's greatest achievement. This has not always been the case, in part because it was lost to Western civilization until its rediscovery in the Renaissance* period. Although *The Republic* has a monumental status within the vast body of Platonic writings, it does not overshadow other dialogues for which Plato is justly famous, such as *Symposium, Protagoras, Apology, Phaedo,* and *Parmenides.* * Even so, *The Republic* certainly represents the most sophisticated synthesis of all of Plato's contributions to Western thought. It also marks the beginning of an important turn towards the constructive and—in the view of critics such as the Austrian-born philosopher Karl Popper*—increasingly authoritarian* political vision developed in *Statesman* and *Laws.*

NOTES

1   Aristotle, *Politics,* trans. Ernest Barker (Oxford: Oxford University Press, 2009), 1264b 26–7.

2   G. R. Ledger, *A Computer Analysis of Plato's Style* (Oxford: Clarendon Press, 1989).

SECTION 3
IMPACT

MODULE 9
THE FIRST RESPONSES

KEY POINTS

- Plato's *The Republic* exercised enormous influence over his immediate successor, Aristotle* of Stagira.

- His influence spread through various philosophical schools in the Hellenistic* period (323–31 B.C.E.) and later, some of which explicitly identified themselves as Platonic.

- The political questions in the dialogue recur in Roman thought, notably informing the Roman philosopher Cicero's* important dialogue, also known as *The Republic*.

Criticism

Plato's *The Republic* exerted huge influence over subsequent chapters of Greek and Roman thinking. This was evident by the very style in which philosophy was pursued—in relaxed collegiate settings in which topics were discussed through many perspectives and debated until a conclusion was reached. By no means all philosophical texts were composed using the dialogue form, but this method stimulated the idea of philosophy as a shared—if competitive—exercise in the pursuit of truth.

Most schools of ancient philosophy presented themselves as similar in structure and spirit to Plato's Academy.* Plato's immediate influence was most pronounced in his successors in the Academy itself. The so-called "Old" Academy continued to champion the metaphysical* and political ideas of their founder until midway through the third century B.C.E., while the "Middle" and "New" Academies, especially under the respective leaderships of Arcesilaus*[1] and Carneades,*[2] took Plato's teachings in the direction of skeptical styles of philosophical thinking.

❝ [Socrates'] inspiration was such that very few philosophers in the Greek, Hellenistic, and Roman worlds (at least until the rise of Christianity and Neoplatonism) did not consider him a predecessor in some significant manner. **❞**

Harold Tarrant, *Plato's First Interpreters*

Although the Academy itself was destroyed by the Romans in 86 B.C.E., the institution was relocated and continued to attract many influential thinkers.

Responses

Ancient Greek and Roman responses to *The Republic* were many and varied. It shows just how far Plato's influence extends that scholars of ancient philosophy apply the labels of "Middle Platonist"* and "Neoplatonist"* to figures well into late antiquity (roughly between 600 and 1000 C.E.). The most celebrated of the thinkers Plato influenced was his best student, Aristotle, who rejected many of his master's foundational positions and developed some of the most insightful criticisms of his work ever written.

In Roman thought, *The Republic* exerted its greatest influence on Cicero's political writings, in particular *De Re Publica* (*On the Republic*), composed between 54 and 50 B.C.E. This text provides a fascinating counterpoint to Plato's work and it was the traditional association of these two seminal contributions to political philosophy that earned Plato's dialogue the name by which we now know it. Cicero is situated self-consciously—and not a little immodestly—in the tradition of political reflection that *The Republic* initiated, although at one point he notes that the vision set out within it is "more desirable than to be hoped for"[3]—in other words, unattainable. Nowhere is this more evident than in the topics to which he devotes attention: the connection between theoretical and practical justice (Book III), the role of education in the formation of citizens (Book IV), and the character of the exemplary citizen (Book V).

One idea in Plato's *The Republic* to which Aristotle strongly objects is the "City-Soul Analogy."* He claims that the degree of biological unity that an individual person possesses cannot be compared to the degree of unity one could reasonably expect of a political community.[4] Aristotle notes that an individual can exist pre-politically; flourishing lives can be led without any place in a political structure and to which no meaningful analogy can be made in political terms. One obvious explanation for Aristotle's abandonment of the "City-Soul Analogy" is that he developed a philosophical anthropology—a philosophy of human nature—that differed in important ways from Plato's. In particular, he rejected the idea that human beings were made up of distinct metaphysical ingredients such as "soul" and "body." Instead, Aristotle proposed that the soul was the structuring principle of the body. Attempting to conceive of the soul as separate from the body was like trying to think of a statue as made up of two components— the blueprint for the sculpture and the rock of marble from which it was cut—that could be pulled apart.

Conflict and Consensus

Something approaching a consensus in relation to Plato's work as a whole—and *The Republic* in particular—emerged from the dominant influence of so-called Neoplatonic philosophy. This movement absorbed many of the metaphysical theses about being and goodness that Plato writes about in *The Republic*. The leading figure in this school was Plotinus, one of the most significant philosophers of late antiquity (the transition between classical antiquity and the medieval period—roughly the second to eighth centuries C.E.).

Neoplatonic thought advanced a complex metaphysical framework built around what has come to be known as "The Great

Chain of Being": a vision of reality as an overflowing "plenitude" (abundance) of goodness from the spiritual into the physical world. The physical world "participates" in the transcendent realm of the One and Intellect (ideas relating, very roughly, to the ultimate source of all reality and the process by which ultimate reality is made available to be understood). These ideas demonstrate a clear debt to the distinctions between the shadowy world of physical reality and the more substantial realm of the forms (especially goodness itself), support for which is given in the "Allegory* of the Divided Line" (509d–511e) and the "Allegory of the Cave" (508b–509c).

This basic structure is one that many subsequent philosophers and theologians* would assume, most notably the great "scholastic"* theologians Thomas Aquinas*[5] and Bonaventure of Bagnoregio*[6] (thinkers who both worked and transmitted their knowledge through principles derived from Plato's method). This was in large part due to the acclaim and authority of a body of writing then thought to be written by an early Christian named Dionysius,* whom Saint Paul,* one of the founders of the early Christian Church, had converted on the Areopagus Hill in Athens (Bible, Acts 17:34).

NOTES

1   Harold Tarrant, *Plato's First Interpreters* (Ithaca, NY: Cornell University Press, 2000), 59–60.

2   Julia Annas, "Plato the Sceptic," in *Oxford Studies in Ancient Philosophy* (Oxford: Oxford University Press, 1992), 43–72.

3   Cicero, *On the Republic*, trans. Niall Rudd (Oxford: Oxford University Press, 1998), 2.52.

4   Aristotle, *On the Soul*, trans. Hugh Lawson-Tancred (London: Penguin, 2004), 2.1.

5   E.g. Thomas Aquinas, *Summa Contra Gentiles*, trans. Vernon Bourke (Notre Dame, IN: University of Notre Dame Press, 1975), 1:37.

6   E.g. Bonaventure, *On the Soul's Journey into God*, trans. Ewert H. Cousins (London: SPCK, 1978), 6.13.

MODULE 10
THE EVOLVING DEBATE

KEY POINTS

- *The Republic* exercised enormous influence over subsequent political philosophers.

- The dialogue can also lay claim to being the first attempt at a form of utopian* literature.

- Plato has been criticized by some thinkers for setting out an overly authoritarian* vision in *The Republic*.

Uses And Problems

Plato's *The Republic* continued to exert an important influence on political philosophers of later periods. Given the extent of its influence, one curious problem affecting *the Republic*'s reception—as well as how it has been used politically in a practical sense—is that the text was effectively lost to Western thinkers from roughly the last quarter of the first millennium and throughout the medieval period. Only in the fourteenth century was *The Republic* translated into Latin.

It seems clear that the fifteenth- to sixteenth-century political philosopher and diplomat Niccolò Machiavelli* has *The Republic* in view when, in his classic work *The Prince* (*Il Principe*) of 1513, he criticizes the idea that the ruler of a state must act justly. Machiavelli argued that there are circumstances when the best interests of the state require a ruler to act unjustly, and *The Prince* would become one of the most influential works in modern political thought. Similarly, the basic conceit of the English social philosopher Thomas More's* *Utopia* (1516)—which describes a fictional, perfect place of that name—owes much to the strategy deployed by the character of Socrates* in *The Republic*. More's *Utopia* was a foundational text for the development of political ideas in the Renaissance* and the early-modern period.

❝ What did Plato mean by justice? I assert that in the *Republic* he used the term 'just' as a synonym for 'that which is in the interest of the best state.' And what is in the interest of the best state? To arrest all change, by the maintenance of a rigid class division and class rule. If I am right in this interpretation, then we should have to say that Plato's demand for justice leaves his political programme at the level of totalitarianism. **❞**

Karl Popper, *The Open Society and Its Enemies, Vol. I: The Spell of Plato*

Schools of Thought

A strong case can be made that *The Republic* has been more formative for the tradition of European literature than any other philosophical text in the classical canon. Since it shaped much of the genre of utopian literature in the West, the inclination in twentieth-century literature to write about totalitarian dystopias must also be included as part of *The Republic*'s legacy. In the major works dealing with this theme, each of the dystopias has features echoing aspects of Plato's ideal city-state. In the British author Aldous Huxley's* *Brave New World* (1931), for instance, reproduction is overseen entirely by the state and non-reproductive sex is encouraged through widespread propaganda in film and through censorship of artistic works that celebrate exclusivity in human relationships.

We find an energetic engagement with Plato's political philosophy in the conservative work of a German Jewish émigré to the United States, the classical philosopher and political theorist Leo Strauss.* Strauss was famously dismissive of the Austrian-born philosopher Karl Popper's* critique of *The Republic* in Popper's *The Open Society and Its Enemies* (1945). He argued that Plato does not intend the dialogue to be a political program that should be practically implemented; rather, Plato's aim is to show *how* to scrutinize and evaluate political constitutions.

This is a stance similar to that of another thinker who held a more sympathetic reading of *The Republic* than Popper, Hans-Georg Gadamer,* the German pioneer of hermeneutics (roughly, an inquiry into the nature of meaning as we find it in literary texts). In "Plato and the Poets" (1934), a lecture delivered at Marburg early in his career, Gadamer argues that Plato devised the utopian model as an interpretative tool to help theorists refine existing political structures and behaviors. The project in *The Republic* is to lay bare political power and its distribution, and to attempt to evaluate the consequences of organizing a city-state in the different ways discussed in the dialogue.

In Current Scholarship

In a contemporary context, much of the debate about *The Republic* surrounds the relationship between Socrates' account of human appetites and desires, and the metaphysical* content of the dialogue. The analysis of human motives in book 4 is logically independent, for example, of the existence of the Form of the Good or the character of the perfect city-state. So are we to interpret *The Republic* primarily as an analysis of the psychology of moral life and the three-part structure of human nature? Or are we to read it as an attempt to work out the best possible ways of organizing society?

The most likely suggestion is that Plato was deliberately seeking to achieve both a lucid philosophical examination of the nature of the soul (how to act justly, what motivates us to act justly, knowledge of objective goodness) *and* a theoretical model for political life. One might argue that the "City-Soul Analogy"* is, in effect, the dominant idea of *The Republic*; it seeks to explain features of political life by drawing comparison with some corresponding feature of moral psychology.

The Republic has bequeathed an important legacy to one of the central debates in contemporary metaphysics: the question of the existence of universals.* These are what Plato refers to as Forms* or

Ideas. This is a question that is discussed in other dialogues—notably *Phaedo*, *Cratylus*, and *Parmenides**—but Plato advances a particularly radical case for the Forms in *The Republic*, according to which there is a Form for every single linguistic term. Every table has as its essence the Form of Table-ness, which is singular; every sophisticated joke is an iteration of the Form of Sophistication. Although no contemporary philosopher would subscribe to this sort of view, several have endorsed a qualified version of the thesis as the best explanation of the fact that there are many features of things that resemble each other. It is implausible to claim that the only way to account for these resemblances is that human beings use the same words to name them.

MODULE 11
IMPACT AND INFLUENCE TODAY

KEY POINTS

- *The Republic* had a notable influence on German and British thinkers of the nineteenth century.

- Plato raises, for the first time in Western thought, the question of an equal distribution of roles between the sexes.

- The dialogue continues to exercise a significant influence within the tradition of political liberalism,* in particular the contemporary debates stimulated by the publication of the social philosopher John Rawls's* *A Theory of Justice*.

Position

Plato's *The Republic* first entered mainstream British thought in the nineteenth century with the declaration by the English ancient historian and parliamentarian George Grote* that *The Republic* was the "grandest" of all Plato's dialogues. His collected edition of Plato and Aristotle was published in three volumes as *Plato and the Other Companions of Socrates* in 1865. Another critically acclaimed historical translation was published shortly afterwards, in 1871, by the Master of Balliol College, Oxford, Benjamin Jowett.* Two reasons for the attraction of *The Republic* to late-Victorian thinkers lay, first, in the emerging public skepticism of religion stimulated by the theories of the English naturalist Charles Darwin,* who offered a scientific account of the processes of natural evolution that posed a great challenge to religious thought; and, second, the enormous social upheavals that shook Britain during the Industrial Revolution, as the country moved from an agricultural to an industrial economy, with all its accompanying social and cultural changes.

❝ Why? Why did I undertake this well-nigh obsessional project based on Plato? Because he is the one we need first and foremost today, for one reason in particular: he launched the idea that conducting our lives in the world assumes that some access to the absolute is available to us ... because the materiality of which we are composed participates ... in the construction of eternal truths. ❞

Alain Badiou, *Plato's Republic: A Dialogue in 16 Chapters*

For the most part, the reception of *The Republic* and Plato's political thought in modern times has been more critical. The latent authoritarianism* of the utopia* Socrates* sketches in *The Republic* (that is, the governmental principles contrary to the citizen's personal liberty), together with the explicitly authoritarian fictional, idealized, state of Magnesia in *Laws*, do not endear themselves to intellectual cultures that have endured the totalitarian* horrors of the twentieth century.[1] Nonetheless, those who identify Plato's political vision as "crypto-communist" or "proto-fascist" risk committing some obvious anachronisms—that is, they identify features or draw parallels that belong to an intellectual and cultural universe far removed in time.

Plato shows no signs of racism—although he would have taken it for granted that only the indigenous citizens of a society could carry out civic roles. As far as gender issues, *The Republic* is momentous: Plato explicitly admits women on an equal basis to the different levels of state governance, including the guardian*-rulers.[2]

The philosopher Karl Popper's* charge that Plato's political philosophy was contrary to the individual's liberty stems, as much as anything else, from his empiricist* distaste for the transcendent Form of the Good to which Plato is committed—that is, Popper's philosophical method was founded on more scientific principles, requiring the analysis of observable evidence. Plato's metaphysical* framework takes moral truths to be as fixed and objective as mathematical ones. But this belief in objective morality is in principle separable from the practical benefits of a utopian model to which civic society should aspire, even if it cannot hope to attain to the ideal in full.

Interaction

For all the criticisms leveled against it, *The Republic* has been positively endorsed by a number of thinkers, especially in the Renaissance* and modern periods. The German American political theorist Leo Strauss* considered some form of the Noble Lie* that Socrates favors in *The Republic* essential to the task of ruling. The Deputy Secretary of Defense in the first Bush Administration, Paul Wolfowitz, a leading neo-conservative thinker (that is, he endorses a right-wing political philosophy sympathetic to, for example, military intervention to protect US interests) is known to have attended the course on Plato that Strauss delivered at the University of Chicago. The Noble Lie, explained by Socrates in book 3 of *The Republic*,[3] is that there *are* circumstances in which a myth, though false, would have a positive impact on the populace by making citizens more committed to each other and more loyal to the state. This is a curious feature of a philosophical work whose author prized the disciplined pursuit of truth above all else, and who rejected the cavalier attitudes to truth of the Sophists.*

The Continuing Debate

The contractarian* or social contract theory* of political justice suggested by the character of Glaucon* in book 2 of *The Republic* continues to exercise an indirect influence in contemporary discussions of political philosophy. John Rawls's *A Theory of Justice* (1971)[4] advocated organizing political communities by establishing principles that would maximize the mutual benefit of individual citizens. Similarly, the political philosopher David Gauthier* has argued that

Glaucon's claim that justice should be founded on consensus among a society's members is more plausible than the alternative that Socrates advances to replace it.[5] Opponents of *The Republic* tend to stake out their territory on the legacy of the English political philosopher Thomas Hobbes* (1588–1679), who was the first thinker to advance a comprehensive and systematic model of political life based on the kind of contractarian principles that are discussed by Glaucon and Adeimantus as they play devil's advocate in book 2 of *The Republic* (they "defend" a contentious idea in order to test arguments against it). The two advocate political realism,* a stance in political philosophy that builds from the central assumption that human nature and political communities are guided by self-interest. This stands in contrast to the metaphysical speculation that Plato urges in *The Republic* and elsewhere, including his theory of Forms* and the more substantial reality that they belong to.

NOTES

1   Lesley Brown, "How Totalitarian is Plato's *Republic*?" in E. N. Ostenfeld, ed., *Essays on Plato's "Republic"* (Aarhus: Aarhus University Press, 1998), 13–27.

2   Julia Annas, "Plato's *Republic* and Feminism," *Philosophy* 51, no. 197 (1976), 307–21; and Gregory Vlastos, "Was Plato a Feminist?" in *Studies in Greek Philosophy II*, ed. D. W. Graham, (Princeton, NJ: Princeton University Press, 1995), 133–43.

3   Plato, *The Republic*, trans. Robin Waterfield (Oxford: Oxford University Press, 1993), 414d–415c.

4   John Rawls, *A Theory of Justice* (Harvard, MA: Harvard University Press, 1971).

5   David Gauthier, *Morals by Agreement* (Oxford: Oxford University Press, 1986).

MODULE 12
WHERE NEXT?

KEY POINTS

- *The Republic* continues to be a central reference point in contemporary political philosophy.

- The Noble Lie* is a philosophical problem most illustrative of the many issues in *The Republic* that continue to be contested in modern political thought.

- It was the focal point of the most famous debate about *The Republic* of the twentieth century—that between the philosopher of science Karl Popper* and the political philosopher Leo Strauss.*

Potential

The legacy of Plato's *The Republic* has been so vast that it naturally continues to feature in many debates on fundamental questions of political philosophy. It is no accident, for instance, that one of the most famous living continental philosophers, the French thinker Alain Badiou,* has recently published a "hypertranslation" of the dialogue[1] (a rewriting in which the references are updated and reinterpreted for our contemporary social predicament). Nevertheless, the disastrous legacy of political utopianism* in the last century—for example the communist project that took shape in Eastern Europe and in North Korea—has made many thinkers reluctant to engage with *The Republic* as anything more than a brilliant but redundant exercise in political thought. Although it is not clear how the dialogue will shape future political ideology, and any such influence will surely be oblique, there is no reason to suppose that it will not endure.

❝The doctrine that an agent's own welfare is the ultimate justification for his morality has become known as eudaimonism ... This view resonates in the proverb 'virtue is its own reward,' and challenges those in the modern world who regard the ultimate justifications for moral behaviour as lying in the interests of others or the demands of a deity. **❞**

Luke Purshouse, *Plato's Republic: A Reader's Guide*

One obvious difference between the contemporary world and the one that *The Republic* influenced in the past is that we are far more interconnected than ever before. Since *The Republic* envisages a relatively self-contained and ethnically monochrome society, its political vision is less relevant in a world where government is increasingly globalized.

Future Directions

One theme in *The Republic* that is likely to shape future discussion is Plato's banishment of poets and artists. The resistance to the arts in *The Republic*—as well as his other utopian vision, the fictional city-state of Magnesia in *Laws*—has earned Plato sharp criticism from a number of contemporary philosophers. Most notable of these, perhaps, is the philosopher of science Karl Popper in the first volume of *The Open Society and Its Enemies* (1945). An equally famous and more sympathetic analysis of Plato's motivation for banishing artists from his ideal political framework is to be found in the English writer Iris Murdoch's* *The Fire and the Sun: Why Plato Banished the Artists* (1977). Murdoch's suggestion, framed in terms of the "Analogy of the Cave," is that Plato believed the great fault of artists is that they perpetuate the illusion of those who live enchained in the cave staring at dancing shadows.

The question of how governments and states convey their political messages was urgent in the twentieth century, a period that witnessed the devastating consequences of propaganda. The question of how private corporations control and manipulate artistic creativity to achieve their commercial ends is increasingly important as the channels for doing so become more extensive.

Summary

The Republic will continue to be an indispensable focal point for students of political philosophy, not least because it is arguably the foundational text for the discipline as a whole. However much contemporary liberalism* conflicts with the conservative thrust of so much of Plato's vision, the work is likely to retain its status. We live in a time when the idea of democratic government is less stable than once hoped, in large part as a result of Western attempts to impose electoral freedom on unprepared regimes using military force or sanctions. Plato's political vision may become increasingly attractive as we contemplate what alternative to democracy would uphold the principles of justice with the same degree of success. Philosophers seeking to resolve some of the most difficult questions in moral philosophy, metaphysics,* and epistemology* will continue to engage with it.

Despite the often bewildering range of philosophical and political topics broached, and the difficulties of elucidating a work that is, after all, nearly 2,500 years old, *The Republic* speaks to us as lucidly and penetratingly as ever. It remains vital if we are to understand the extraordinary variety and richness of the Western intellectual tradition that emerged in its wake.

NOTES

1   Alain Badiou, *Plato's* Republic: *A Dialogue in 16 Chapters* (New York: Columbia University Press, 2012).

GLOSSARY

GLOSSARY OF TERMS

Aesthetics: a branch of philosophical inquiry dealing with questions of beauty, taste, and appearance.

Allegories: stories that convey meaning and ideas and highlight actual truth through symbol and fiction.

Authoritarian: a system of government in central authority that operates at the expense of individual liberty.

Academy: an institution of higher learning founded by Plato circa 387 B.C.E.

City-Soul analogy: Plato theorized that the soul was made of three parts: a rational part, which seeks truth; a spirited part, which desires honor and righteousness; and an appetitive part, which lusts after money and other rewards. These three parts are analogous with the three parts of society: producers (craftsmen, farmers, artisans, etc.), auxiliaries (warriors), and guardians (rulers).

Colonization: the process of settling foreign territories.

Communitarian: an approach to social organization that emphasizes the relation of the individual to the community.

Contractarianism: a political theory according to which political legitimacy and justice consist in the mutual agreement of the governed and those who govern them, also known as social contract theory.

Dualism: the conceptual division of a whole into two constituent parts. The idea is often split into subdivisions such as moral dualism, which argues the existence of a conflict between the benevolent and the malevolent, and ontological dualism, which argues that the world is divided into two separate categories such as yin and yang.

Elenchus: the method, associated with Socrates, of arriving at the truth through the asking of questions.

Empiricism: an approach to philosophical and scientific inquiry in which deduction is founded on the analysis of observable evidence.

Epistemology: the theory and philosophy of knowledge.

Forms: things that cannot be sensed but that are, according to Plato, more real than things that can be sensed.

Guardians: the word "guardians" as Plato used it meant the social class who would rule a city; they were also known as philosopher-kings.

Hellenistic period: the name given to the peak of Greek influence and power. The period began with the death of Alexander the Great in 323 B.C.E. and lasted until the emergence of the Roman Empire as signified by the Battle of Actium in 31 B.C.E.

Hetairai: educated, nominally independent women, with a particular legal status, who provided companionship to men.

Liberal: a word with many connotations and usages in fields as diverse as economics, politics, and religion. A "liberal" political philosophy is usually understood to be founded on notions of personal liberty and equality.

Macat Analysis of **Plato's** *The Republic*

Liberalism: a philosophy that promotes the individual as the most important social unit. It also places great weight on the protection of individual rights and freedoms, including economic and property rights.

Libertarian: someone who adheres to a political philosophy according to which the role of a government should be reduced to a bare minimum in the functioning of the state and the lives of the nation's citizens.

Machtpolitik: a German term for power-politics, a form of individual and international relations based on self-interest.

Metaethics: the philosophical study of the fundamental character of goodness and moral obligation.

Metaphysics: a branch of philosophy dealing with fundamental questions about the nature of existence such as time, being, knowledge, and so on.

Metic: a resident of Ancient Athens who did not have citizen rights in the *polis* itself.

Middle Platonism: a phase in the development of Platonic philosophy from the late first century B.C.E. to around the third century C.E.

Might-is-right: a pejorative English phrase used to describe the illegitimate or amoral abuse of power over individuals or communities.

Neoplatonism: the final phase in the development of Platonic philosophy, which lasted from the third century C.E. to the closure of the Academy in 529 C.E.

Noble Lie: a political message, typically framed as a religious story or myth, that is untrue but considered justified for upholding the unity and harmony of a society.

Pedagogy: theories about the best ways of conducting education.

Oligarchy: government by a small group of people of high status.

Peloponnesian War (431–404 B.C.E.): a conflict in three phases between Athens and her empire and the Peloponnesian League led by Sparta that ended in the defeat of Athens and the collapse of her empire.

Polis: the Greek term for a city-state (or for the actual citizenry of a city-state), the principal form of political organization in Classical Greece

Pre-Socratics: philosophers and natural scientists who lived before Socrates. Socrates died in 399 B.C.E., so influential thinkers such as Plato and Aristotle are not pre-Socratic.

Realism: a political philosophy founded on the idea that people and nations are motivated to act, above all, by self-interest.

Realpolitik: a German term for a theory of politics and diplomacy, according to which power is to be exercised irrespective of ideological or moral considerations.

Relativism: the idea that it is impossible to arrive at certainties (frequently ethical) since, given that contexts change, these things cannot be absolute.

Renaissance: A period roughly covering the fourteenth to the seventeenth centuries, when European culture reinvigorated itself with a turn towards the forms of Classical Greece and Rome. The onset of the Renaissance was not uniform and its earliest origins are to be found in Italy during the Renaissance's "Latin phase." From there it eventually spread across Europe.

Rhetoric: the art of speaking publicly to move and motivate an audience. Plato felt that the art of rhetoric was misused by the philosophical group known as the Sophists.

Scholasticism: an approach to the production and transmission of knowledge based on Plato's method, particularly his means of arriving at an argument through framing ideas in a dialogue; a method of teaching of the medieval period, influential until the seventeenth century.

Social contract theory: a political theory, according to which political legitimacy and justice consist in the mutual agreement of the governed and those who govern them, also known as contractarianism.

Socratic dialectic: the philosophical method most associated with Socrates, in which an initial claim ("thesis") is advanced and subsequently disputed by a counter-claim ("antithesis") with the aim of attaining a more persuasive concluding claim ("synthesis").

Sparta: a city-state in the Peloponnese and Athens's principal rival in the Peloponnesian War.

Sophists: a group of largely itinerant teachers in Classical Greece who taught rhetoric for money.

Theologians: people who conduct systematic study into religious matters.

Thirty Tyrants: a group of elite politicians installed to rule Athens in the wake of her defeat at the hands of Sparta in 404 B.C.E. and who ruled for a brief but bloody and corrupt 13 months.

Totalitarianism: a system of government in which the citizen is utterly subject to the state.

Universals: characteristics or underlying qualities that are common to all particular examples of a certain thing.

Utopian: a word describing the impossible perfection of a place that, properly speaking, exists only in the imagination.

PEOPLE MENTIONED IN THE TEXT

Adeimantus of Collytus (circa 432–382 B.C.E.) was an Ancient Athenian, the younger brother of Glaucon and elder brother of Plato.

Alexander the Great (circa 356–323 B.C.E.) was a pupil of Aristotle, King of Macedon, and one of history's greatest military commanders.

Anaximander (circa 610–circa 546 B.C.E.) was a pre-Socratic philosopher who was the first philosopher known to have to written his work down, although it survives only in fragments. He was an early advocate of scientific methods.

Anaximenes (circa 585–circa 528 B.C.E.) was a pre-Socratic philosopher and student of Anaximander. He believed, as Thales did, that there was one originating element which underlay all reality. Anaximenes believed this element was air.

Thomas Aquinas (1225–74), born Tommaso d'Aquino, was an Italian Dominican theologian, recognized as a preeminent medieval philosopher and founder of the Thomist school of thought. He was canonized in 1323.

Arcesilaus (316–241 B.C.E.) was a founder of the Middle Academy, a school originally founded by Plato.

Aristotle of Stagira (384–322 B.C.E.) was a Greek philosopher and scientist, one of the most influential philosophers in the Western tradition. He was a student at Plato's Academy.

Alain Badiou (b. 1937) is a distinguished French philosopher, politically left wing. Among his many works, he has published a "hypertranslation" of Plato's *Republic* (a reinterpretation in which the original work's references and political history have been updated for a modern context).

George Berkeley (1685–1753) was an Irish philosopher and the Bishop of Cloyne. He was a leading exponent of the British empiricist tradition.

Boethius (480–524 C.E.) was a Roman consul after the deposition of the last Roman emperor. He wrote the *Consolation of Philosophy*, one of the most influential works of the medieval period.

Bonaventure of Bagnoregio (1221–74), born Giovanni di Fidanza, was an Italian theologian and Bishop of Albano, canonized in 1482.

Carneades (214–129 B.C.E.) was a member of the Academic skeptical school, who doubted both sense-experience and reasoning.

Cephalus (circa fifth century B.C.E.) was the son of Lysanias from Syracuse, a wealthy metic and father of the orator Lysias.

Cicero (106–43 B.C.E.) was a Roman philosopher, lawyer, orator, politician, and philosopher.

Cleitophon (fifth to fourth century B.C.E.) was an Athenian politician. He was a key player in the oligarchic coup in Athens in 411 B.C.E.

Charles Darwin (1809–82) was an English naturalist who proposed that all species of life have descended from common ancestors, and that evolution resulted from evolution by a process of natural selection.

Dionysius the Areopagite (first century C.E.) was converted to Christianity by St. Paul, as mentioned in the Bible (Acts 17:34). He reputedly became the first Bishop of Athens.

Dionysius I of Syracuse (circa 432–367 B.C.E.) was a Greek tyrant of Syracuse, a city on the island of Sicily.

Hans-Georg Gadamer (1900–2002) was a German philosopher who developed the theory of hermeneutics (an inquiry into the nature of meaning as we find it in literary texts) in his most celebrated work *Truth and Method* (1960).

David Gauthier (b. 1932) is a Canadian American political philosopher and advocate of a neo-Hobbesian social contract theory of morality.

Glaucon (circa 445–fourth century B.C.E.) was an Ancient Athenian and the elder brother of Plato and Adeimantus.

Gorgias of Leontium (circa 485–circa 380 B.C.E.) was a Greek Sophist, pre-Socratic philosopher, and rhetorician.

George Grote (1794–1871) was a historian of Ancient Greece and an English politician.

Heraclitus of Ephesus (circa 535–475 B.C.E.) was a pre-Socratic philosopher notable for his theory that all things are in a state of flux. Although none of his works survive, we know that he was the author of *On Nature*—a generic title used by many of the early philosophers covering cosmology, physics, morality, and epistemology.

Thomas Hobbes (1588–1679) was an English political philosopher and one of the founders of social contract theory.

David Hume (1714–76) was a Scottish Enlightenment philosopher, historian, economist, and essayist.

Aldous Huxley (1894–1963) was a British novelist and essayist.

Benjamin Jowett (1817–93) was an influential teacher, theologian, and administrative reformer at the University of Oxford. He was also the translator of an influential edition of Plato's dialogues.

Niccolò Machiavelli (1469–1527) was a highly influential Renaissance diplomat, politician, political theorist, and author of *The Prince* (*Il Principe*) (1513).

Thomas More (1478–1535) was an English diplomat and social theorist; he is the author of the influential work *Utopia*.

Iris Murdoch (1919–99) was a British novelist and philosopher.

Robert Nozick (1938–2002) was an American political philosopher, libertarian, and professor at Harvard University.

Parmenides of Elea (circa fifth century B.C.E.) was a pre-Socratic philosopher and founder of the Eleatic school of philosophy.

Paul the Apostle/Saint Paul (circa 5–circa 67 C.E.), formerly Saul of Tarsus, was an apostle of Jesus Christ and author of several writings of the New Testament.

Plotinus (circa 205–70 C.E.) was a philosopher, probably of Roman descent.

Polemarchus (circa fifth century B.C.E.**)** was an Ancient Athenian philosopher and son of Cephalus, who was executed by the Thirty Tyrants in 404 B.C.E.

Karl Popper (1902–94) was an Austrian émigré philosopher of science.

Porphyry (circa 234–305 C.E**)** was a philosopher of the Roman period; a student of Plotinus.

Protagoras of Abdera (490–420 B.C.E.**)** was a pre-Socratic philosopher and Sophist.

John Rawls (1921–2002) was an American political philosopher and professor at Harvard University.

Bertrand Russell (1872–1970) was a British analytic philosopher, noted for his activities as a mathematician, historian, and social critic. His most famous work is *Principia Mathematica* (1910–13), written with Alfred North Whitehead, which attempted to systematize mathematical study along the lines of logic.

Michael Sandel (b. 1953) is an American political philosopher and communitarian philosopher.

Amartya Sen (b. 1933) is Indian economist and philosopher. He was awarded the Nobel Memorial Prize in Economic Sciences in 1998 for his contribution to welfare economics.

Socrates (470–399 B.C.E.**)** was an Ancient Athenian and one of the founders of Western philosophy.

Leo Strauss (1899–1973) was a German American philosopher, classicist, and professor at the University of Chicago.

Thales (circa 624–546 B.C.E.) is widely regarded as the first philosopher in the Greek tradition. He proposed that water was the originating principle of all matter.

Thrasymachus of Chalcedon (circa 450–circa 400 B.C.E.) was a Greek sophist and rhetorician.

Thucydides (circa 460–circa 400 B.C.E.) was an Athenian historian, political philosopher, and general. He is noted as the author of *History of the Peloponnesian War*, a book regarded as foundational to the modern discipline of history.

Alfred North Whitehead (1861–1947) was an English philosopher and mathematician who co-wrote *Principia Mathematica* (1910–13) with Bertrand Russell. Subsequently he undertook groundbreaking work in metaphysics known as process philosophy.

Paul Wolfowitz (b. 1943) is a former president of the World Bank and US deputy secretary of defense. He is notable for being a prominent neoconservative thinker.

Xenophon (circa 430–354 B.C.E.) was an Ancient Greek historian, soldier, and mercenary.

WORKS CITED

WORKS CITED

Annas, Julia. "Plato's *Republic* and Feminism." *Philosophy* 51, no. 197 (1976): 307–21.

"Plato the Sceptic." In *Oxford Studies in Ancient Philosophy*, 43–72. Oxford: Oxford University Press, 1992.

Aquinas, Thomas. *Summa Contra Gentiles*. Translated by Vernon J. Bourke. Notre Dame, IN: University of Notre Dame Press, 1975.

Aristotle, *On the Soul*. Translated by Hugh Lawson-Tancred. London: Penguin, 2004.

Politics. Translated by Ernest Barker. Oxford: Oxford University Press, 2009.

Badiou, Alain. *Plato's* Republic*: A Dialogue in 16 Chapters*. New York: Columbia University Press, 2012

Bonaventure, *On the Soul's Journey into God*. Translated by Ewert H. Cousins. London: SPCK, 1978.

Brown, Lesley. "How Totalitarian is Plato's *Republic*?" In *Essays on Plato's "Republic,"* edited by E. N. Ostenfeld, 13–27. Aarhus: Aarhus University Press, 1998.

"Glaucon's Challenge, Rational Egoism and Ordinary Morality." In *Pursuing the Good: Ethics and Metaphysics in Plato's Republic,* edited by Douglas Cairns, Fritz-Gregor Herrmann and Terry Penner, 42–60. Edinburgh: Edinburgh University Press, 2007.

Cicero, *On the Republic*. Translated by Niall Rudd. Oxford: Oxford University Press, 1998.

Davidson, James. *Courtesans and Fishcakes: Consuming Passions in Classical Athens.* London: Harper Collins, 1997.

Gadamer, Hans-Georg. "Plato and the Poets." In *Dialogue and Dialectic: Eight Hermeneutical Studies on Plato*, translated by P. Christopher Smith. New Haven, CT: Yale University Press, 1980.

Gauthier, David. *Morals by Agreement.* Oxford: Oxford University Press, 1986.

Hornblower, Simon. "Greece: The History of the Classical Period." In *The Oxford History of Greece and the Hellenistic World,* edited by John Boardman, Jasper Griffin, and Oswyn Murray, 142–76. Oxford: Oxford University Press, 2001.

Kraut, Richard. "The Defense of Justice in Plato's *Republic*." In *Plato's Republic: Critical Essays*, edited by Richard Kraut, 1–16. New York: Rowman and Littlefield, 1997.

Ledger, G. R. *A Computer Analysis of Plato's Style.* Oxford: Clarendon Press, 1989.

Machiavelli, Niccolò. *The Prince* (*Il Principe*). Translated by Daniel Donno. New York: Bantam Classics, 1984.

More, Thomas. *Utopia.* Translated by Paul Turner. London: Penguin Books, 1965.

Murdoch, Iris. *The Fire and the Sun: Why Plato Banished the Artists.* Oxford: Oxford University Press, 1977.

Nozick, Robert. *Anarchy, State, and Utopia.* New York: Basic Books, 1974.

Plato, *The Republic*. Translated by Robin Waterfield. Oxford: Oxford University Press, 1993.

Popper, Karl. *The Open Society and Its Enemies, Volume I: The Spell of Plato.* London: Routledge, 1945.

Rawls, John. *A Theory of Justice.* Harvard, MA: Harvard University Press, 1971.

Sachs, David. "A Fallacy in Plato's *Republic*." *Philosophical Review* 72, no. 2 (1963): 141–58.

Sandel, Michael J. *Liberalism and the Limits of Justice.* Cambridge: Cambridge University Press, 1982.

Sen, Amartya. *The Idea of Justice.* Harvard, MA: Harvard University Press 2009.

Tarrant, Harold. *Plato's First Interpreters.* Ithaca, NY: Cornell University Press, 2000.

Thucydides. *History of the Peloponnesian War*. Translated by Rex Warner. New York: Penguin Classics, 1972.

Vlastos, Gregory. "Was Plato a Feminist?" In *Studies in Greek Philosophy II,* edited by D. W. Graham, 133–43. Princeton, NJ: Princeton University Press, 1995.

Whitehead, Alfred North. *Process and Reality.* Cambridge: Cambridge University Press, 1929.

Xenophon, *Apology.* Translated by O. J. Todd. Harvard, MA: Harvard University Press, 2003.

THE MACAT LIBRARY
BY DISCIPLINE

The Macat Library By Discipline

AFRICANA STUDIES

Chinua Achebe's *An Image of Africa: Racism in Conrad's Heart of Darkness*
W. E. B. Du Bois's *The Souls of Black Folk*
Zora Neale Huston's *Characteristics of Negro Expression*
Martin Luther King Jr's *Why We Can't Wait*
Toni Morrison's *Playing in the Dark: Whiteness in the American Literary Imagination*

ANTHROPOLOGY

Arjun Appadurai's *Modernity at Large: Cultural Dimensions of Globalisation*
Philippe Ariès's *Centuries of Childhood*
Franz Boas's *Race, Language and Culture*
Kim Chan & Renée Mauborgne's *Blue Ocean Strategy*
Jared Diamond's *Guns, Germs & Steel: the Fate of Human Societies*
Jared Diamond's *Collapse: How Societies Choose to Fail or Survive*
E. E. Evans-Pritchard's *Witchcraft, Oracles and Magic Among the Azande*
James Ferguson's *The Anti-Politics Machine*
Clifford Geertz's *The Interpretation of Cultures*
David Graeber's *Debt: the First 5000 Years*
Karen Ho's *Liquidated: An Ethnography of Wall Street*
Geert Hofstede's *Culture's Consequences: Comparing Values, Behaviors, Institutes and Organizations across Nations*
Claude Lévi-Strauss's *Structural Anthropology*
Jay Macleod's *Ain't No Makin' It: Aspirations and Attainment in a Low-Income Neighborhood*
Saba Mahmood's *The Politics of Piety: The Islamic Revival and the Feminist Subject*
Marcel Mauss's *The Gift*

BUSINESS

Jean Lave & Etienne Wenger's *Situated Learning*
Theodore Levitt's *Marketing Myopia*
Burton G. Malkiel's *A Random Walk Down Wall Street*
Douglas McGregor's *The Human Side of Enterprise*
Michael Porter's *Competitive Strategy: Creating and Sustaining Superior Performance*
John Kotter's *Leading Change*
C. K. Prahalad & Gary Hamel's *The Core Competence of the Corporation*

CRIMINOLOGY

Michelle Alexander's *The New Jim Crow: Mass Incarceration in the Age of Colorblindness*
Michael R. Gottfredson & Travis Hirschi's *A General Theory of Crime*
Richard Herrnstein & Charles A. Murray's *The Bell Curve: Intelligence and Class Structure in American Life*
Elizabeth Loftus's *Eyewitness Testimony*
Jay Macleod's *Ain't No Makin' It: Aspirations and Attainment in a Low-Income Neighborhood*
Philip Zimbardo's *The Lucifer Effect*

ECONOMICS

Janet Abu-Lughod's *Before European Hegemony*
Ha-Joon Chang's *Kicking Away the Ladder*
David Brion Davis's *The Problem of Slavery in the Age of Revolution*
Milton Friedman's *The Role of Monetary Policy*
Milton Friedman's *Capitalism and Freedom*
David Graeber's *Debt: the First 5000 Years*
Friedrich Hayek's *The Road to Serfdom*
Karen Ho's *Liquidated: An Ethnography of Wall Street*

John Maynard Keynes's *The General Theory of Employment, Interest and Money*
Charles P. Kindleberger's *Manias, Panics and Crashes*
Robert Lucas's *Why Doesn't Capital Flow from Rich to Poor Countries?*
Burton G. Malkiel's *A Random Walk Down Wall Street*
Thomas Robert Malthus's *An Essay on the Principle of Population*
Karl Marx's *Capital*
Thomas Piketty's *Capital in the Twenty-First Century*
Amartya Sen's *Development as Freedom*
Adam Smith's *The Wealth of Nations*
Nassim Nicholas Taleb's *The Black Swan: The Impact of the Highly Improbable*
Amos Tversky's & Daniel Kahneman's *Judgment under Uncertainty: Heuristics and Biases*
Mahbub Ul Haq's *Reflections on Human Development*
Max Weber's *The Protestant Ethic and the Spirit of Capitalism*

FEMINISM AND GENDER STUDIES

Judith Butler's *Gender Trouble*
Simone De Beauvoir's *The Second Sex*
Michel Foucault's *History of Sexuality*
Betty Friedan's *The Feminine Mystique*
Saba Mahmood's *The Politics of Piety: The Islamic Revival and the Feminist Subject*
Joan Wallach Scott's *Gender and the Politics of History*
Mary Wollstonecraft's *A Vindication of the Rights of Woman*
Virginia Woolf's *A Room of One's Own*

GEOGRAPHY

The Brundtland Report's *Our Common Future*
Rachel Carson's *Silent Spring*
Charles Darwin's *On the Origin of Species*
James Ferguson's *The Anti-Politics Machine*
Jane Jacobs's *The Death and Life of Great American Cities*
James Lovelock's *Gaia: A New Look at Life on Earth*
Amartya Sen's *Development as Freedom*
Mathis Wackernagel & William Rees's *Our Ecological Footprint*

HISTORY

Janet Abu-Lughod's *Before European Hegemony*
Benedict Anderson's *Imagined Communities*
Bernard Bailyn's *The Ideological Origins of the American Revolution*
Hanna Batatu's *The Old Social Classes And The Revolutionary Movements Of Iraq*
Christopher Browning's *Ordinary Men: Reserve Police Batallion 101 and the Final Solution in Poland*
Edmund Burke's *Reflections on the Revolution in France*
William Cronon's *Nature's Metropolis: Chicago And The Great West*
Alfred W. Crosby's *The Columbian Exchange*
Hamid Dabashi's *Iran: A People Interrupted*
David Brion Davis's *The Problem of Slavery in the Age of Revolution*
Nathalie Zemon Davis's *The Return of Martin Guerre*
Jared Diamond's *Guns, Germs & Steel: the Fate of Human Societies*
Frank Dikotter's *Mao's Great Famine*
John W Dower's *War Without Mercy: Race And Power In The Pacific War*
W. E. B. Du Bois's *The Souls of Black Folk*
Richard J. Evans's *In Defence of History*
Lucien Febvre's *The Problem of Unbelief in the 16th Century*
Sheila Fitzpatrick's *Everyday Stalinism*

The Macat Library By Discipline

Eric Foner's *Reconstruction: America's Unfinished Revolution, 1863-1877*
Michel Foucault's *Discipline and Punish*
Michel Foucault's *History of Sexuality*
Francis Fukuyama's *The End of History and the Last Man*
John Lewis Gaddis's *We Now Know: Rethinking Cold War History*
Ernest Gellner's *Nations and Nationalism*
Eugene Genovese's *Roll, Jordan, Roll: The World the Slaves Made*
Carlo Ginzburg's *The Night Battles*
Daniel Goldhagen's *Hitler's Willing Executioners*
Jack Goldstone's *Revolution and Rebellion in the Early Modern World*
Antonio Gramsci's *The Prison Notebooks*
Alexander Hamilton, John Jay & James Madison's *The Federalist Papers*
Christopher Hill's *The World Turned Upside Down*
Carole Hillenbrand's *The Crusades: Islamic Perspectives*
Thomas Hobbes's *Leviathan*
Eric Hobsbawm's *The Age Of Revolution*
John A. Hobson's *Imperialism: A Study*
Albert Hourani's *History of the Arab Peoples*
Samuel P. Huntington's *The Clash of Civilizations and the Remaking of World Order*
C. L. R. James's *The Black Jacobins*
Tony Judt's *Postwar: A History of Europe Since 1945*
Ernst Kantorowicz's *The King's Two Bodies: A Study in Medieval Political Theology*
Paul Kennedy's *The Rise and Fall of the Great Powers*
Ian Kershaw's *The "Hitler Myth": Image and Reality in the Third Reich*
John Maynard Keynes's *The General Theory of Employment, Interest and Money*
Charles P. Kindleberger's *Manias, Panics and Crashes*
Martin Luther King Jr's *Why We Can't Wait*
Henry Kissinger's *World Order: Reflections on the Character of Nations and the Course of History*
Thomas Kuhn's *The Structure of Scientific Revolutions*
Georges Lefebvre's *The Coming of the French Revolution*
John Locke's *Two Treatises of Government*
Niccolò Machiavelli's *The Prince*
Thomas Robert Malthus's *An Essay on the Principle of Population*
Mahmood Mamdani's *Citizen and Subject: Contemporary Africa And The Legacy Of Late Colonialism*
Karl Marx's *Capital*
Stanley Milgram's *Obedience to Authority*
John Stuart Mill's *On Liberty*
Thomas Paine's *Common Sense*
Thomas Paine's *Rights of Man*
Geoffrey Parker's *Global Crisis: War, Climate Change and Catastrophe in the Seventeenth Century*
Jonathan Riley-Smith's *The First Crusade and the Idea of Crusading*
Jean-Jacques Rousseau's *The Social Contract*
Joan Wallach Scott's *Gender and the Politics of History*
Theda Skocpol's *States and Social Revolutions*
Adam Smith's *The Wealth of Nations*
Timothy Snyder's *Bloodlands: Europe Between Hitler and Stalin*
Sun Tzu's *The Art of War*
Keith Thomas's *Religion and the Decline of Magic*
Thucydides's *The History of the Peloponnesian War*
Frederick Jackson Turner's *The Significance of the Frontier in American History*
Odd Arne Westad's *The Global Cold War: Third World Interventions And The Making Of Our Times*

LITERATURE

Chinua Achebe's *An Image of Africa: Racism in Conrad's Heart of Darkness*
Roland Barthes's *Mythologies*
Homi K. Bhabha's *The Location of Culture*
Judith Butler's *Gender Trouble*
Simone De Beauvoir's *The Second Sex*
Ferdinand De Saussure's *Course in General Linguistics*
T. S. Eliot's *The Sacred Wood: Essays on Poetry and Criticism*
Zora Neale Huston's *Characteristics of Negro Expression*
Toni Morrison's *Playing in the Dark: Whiteness in the American Literary Imagination*
Edward Said's *Orientalism*
Gayatri Chakravorty Spivak's *Can the Subaltern Speak?*
Mary Wollstonecraft's *A Vindication of the Rights of Women*
Virginia Woolf's *A Room of One's Own*

PHILOSOPHY

Elizabeth Anscombe's *Modern Moral Philosophy*
Hannah Arendt's *The Human Condition*
Aristotle's *Metaphysics*
Aristotle's *Nicomachean Ethics*
Edmund Gettier's *Is Justified True Belief Knowledge?*
Georg Wilhelm Friedrich Hegel's *Phenomenology of Spirit*
David Hume's *Dialogues Concerning Natural Religion*
David Hume's *The Enquiry for Human Understanding*
Immanuel Kant's *Religion within the Boundaries of Mere Reason*
Immanuel Kant's *Critique of Pure Reason*
Søren Kierkegaard's *The Sickness Unto Death*
Søren Kierkegaard's *Fear and Trembling*
C. S. Lewis's *The Abolition of Man*
Alasdair MacIntyre's *After Virtue*
Marcus Aurelius's *Meditations*
Friedrich Nietzsche's *On the Genealogy of Morality*
Friedrich Nietzsche's *Beyond Good and Evil*
Plato's *Republic*
Plato's *Symposium*
Jean-Jacques Rousseau's *The Social Contract*
Gilbert Ryle's *The Concept of Mind*
Baruch Spinoza's *Ethics*
Sun Tzu's *The Art of War*
Ludwig Wittgenstein's *Philosophical Investigations*

POLITICS

Benedict Anderson's *Imagined Communities*
Aristotle's *Politics*
Bernard Bailyn's *The Ideological Origins of the American Revolution*
Edmund Burke's *Reflections on the Revolution in France*
John C. Calhoun's *A Disquisition on Government*
Ha-Joon Chang's *Kicking Away the Ladder*
Hamid Dabashi's *Iran: A People Interrupted*
Hamid Dabashi's *Theology of Discontent: The Ideological Foundation of the Islamic Revolution in Iran*
Robert Dahl's *Democracy and its Critics*
Robert Dahl's *Who Governs?*
David Brion Davis's *The Problem of Slavery in the Age of Revolution*

The Macat Library By Discipline

Alexis De Tocqueville's *Democracy in America*
James Ferguson's *The Anti-Politics Machine*
Frank Dikotter's *Mao's Great Famine*
Sheila Fitzpatrick's *Everyday Stalinism*
Eric Foner's *Reconstruction: America's Unfinished Revolution, 1863-1877*
Milton Friedman's *Capitalism and Freedom*
Francis Fukuyama's *The End of History and the Last Man*
John Lewis Gaddis's *We Now Know: Rethinking Cold War History*
Ernest Gellner's *Nations and Nationalism*
David Graeber's *Debt: the First 5000 Years*
Antonio Gramsci's *The Prison Notebooks*
Alexander Hamilton, John Jay & James Madison's *The Federalist Papers*
Friedrich Hayek's *The Road to Serfdom*
Christopher Hill's *The World Turned Upside Down*
Thomas Hobbes's *Leviathan*
John A. Hobson's *Imperialism: A Study*
Samuel P. Huntington's *The Clash of Civilizations and the Remaking of World Order*
Tony Judt's *Postwar: A History of Europe Since 1945*
David C. Kang's *China Rising: Peace, Power and Order in East Asia*
Paul Kennedy's *The Rise and Fall of Great Powers*
Robert Keohane's *After Hegemony*
Martin Luther King Jr.'s *Why We Can't Wait*
Henry Kissinger's *World Order: Reflections on the Character of Nations and the Course of History*
John Locke's *Two Treatises of Government*
Niccolò Machiavelli's *The Prince*
Thomas Robert Malthus's *An Essay on the Principle of Population*
Mahmood Mamdani's *Citizen and Subject: Contemporary Africa And The Legacy Of Late Colonialism*
Karl Marx's *Capital*
John Stuart Mill's *On Liberty*
John Stuart Mill's *Utilitarianism*
Hans Morgenthau's *Politics Among Nations*
Thomas Paine's *Common Sense*
Thomas Paine's *Rights of Man*
Thomas Piketty's *Capital in the Twenty-First Century*
Robert D. Putman's *Bowling Alone*
John Rawls's *Theory of Justice*
Jean-Jacques Rousseau's *The Social Contract*
Theda Skocpol's *States and Social Revolutions*
Adam Smith's *The Wealth of Nations*
Sun Tzu's *The Art of War*
Henry David Thoreau's *Civil Disobedience*
Thucydides's *The History of the Peloponnesian War*
Kenneth Waltz's *Theory of International Politics*
Max Weber's *Politics as a Vocation*
Odd Arne Westad's *The Global Cold War: Third World Interventions And The Making Of Our Times*

POSTCOLONIAL STUDIES

Roland Barthes's *Mythologies*
Frantz Fanon's *Black Skin, White Masks*
Homi K. Bhabha's *The Location of Culture*
Gustavo Gutiérrez's *A Theology of Liberation*
Edward Said's *Orientalism*
Gayatri Chakravorty Spivak's *Can the Subaltern Speak?*

PSYCHOLOGY

Gordon Allport's *The Nature of Prejudice*
Alan Baddeley & Graham Hitch's *Aggression: A Social Learning Analysis*
Albert Bandura's *Aggression: A Social Learning Analysis*
Leon Festinger's *A Theory of Cognitive Dissonance*
Sigmund Freud's *The Interpretation of Dreams*
Betty Friedan's *The Feminine Mystique*
Michael R. Gottfredson & Travis Hirschi's *A General Theory of Crime*
Eric Hoffer's *The True Believer: Thoughts on the Nature of Mass Movements*
William James's *Principles of Psychology*
Elizabeth Loftus's *Eyewitness Testimony*
A. H. Maslow's *A Theory of Human Motivation*
Stanley Milgram's *Obedience to Authority*
Steven Pinker's *The Better Angels of Our Nature*
Oliver Sacks's *The Man Who Mistook His Wife For a Hat*
Richard Thaler & Cass Sunstein's *Nudge: Improving Decisions About Health, Wealth and Happiness*
Amos Tversky's *Judgment under Uncertainty: Heuristics and Biases*
Philip Zimbardo's *The Lucifer Effect*

SCIENCE

Rachel Carson's *Silent Spring*
William Cronon's *Nature's Metropolis: Chicago And The Great West*
Alfred W. Crosby's *The Columbian Exchange*
Charles Darwin's *On the Origin of Species*
Richard Dawkin's *The Selfish Gene*
Thomas Kuhn's *The Structure of Scientific Revolutions*
Geoffrey Parker's *Global Crisis: War, Climate Change and Catastrophe in the Seventeenth Century*
Mathis Wackernagel & William Rees's *Our Ecological Footprint*

SOCIOLOGY

Michelle Alexander's *The New Jim Crow: Mass Incarceration in the Age of Colorblindness*
Gordon Allport's *The Nature of Prejudice*
Albert Bandura's *Aggression: A Social Learning Analysis*
Hanna Batatu's *The Old Social Classes And The Revolutionary Movements Of Iraq*
Ha-Joon Chang's *Kicking Away the Ladder*
W. E. B. Du Bois's *The Souls of Black Folk*
Émile Durkheim's *On Suicide*
Frantz Fanon's *Black Skin, White Masks*
Frantz Fanon's *The Wretched of the Earth*
Eric Foner's *Reconstruction: America's Unfinished Revolution, 1863-1877*
Eugene Genovese's *Roll, Jordan, Roll: The World the Slaves Made*
Jack Goldstone's *Revolution and Rebellion in the Early Modern World*
Antonio Gramsci's *The Prison Notebooks*
Richard Herrnstein & Charles A Murray's *The Bell Curve: Intelligence and Class Structure in American Life*
Eric Hoffer's *The True Believer: Thoughts on the Nature of Mass Movements*
Jane Jacobs's *The Death and Life of Great American Cities*
Robert Lucas's *Why Doesn't Capital Flow from Rich to Poor Countries?*
Jay Macleod's *Ain't No Makin' It: Aspirations and Attainment in a Low Income Neighborhood*
Elaine May's *Homeward Bound: American Families in the Cold War Era*
Douglas McGregor's *The Human Side of Enterprise*
C. Wright Mills's *The Sociological Imagination*

Thomas Piketty's *Capital in the Twenty-First Century*
Robert D. Putman's *Bowling Alone*
David Riesman's *The Lonely Crowd: A Study of the Changing American Character*
Edward Said's *Orientalism*
Joan Wallach Scott's *Gender and the Politics of History*
Theda Skocpol's *States and Social Revolutions*
Max Weber's *The Protestant Ethic and the Spirit of Capitalism*

THEOLOGY

Augustine's *Confessions*
Benedict's *Rule of St Benedict*
Gustavo Gutiérrez's *A Theology of Liberation*
Carole Hillenbrand's *The Crusades: Islamic Perspectives*
David Hume's *Dialogues Concerning Natural Religion*
Immanuel Kant's *Religion within the Boundaries of Mere Reason*
Ernst Kantorowicz's *The King's Two Bodies: A Study in Medieval Political Theology*
Søren Kierkegaard's *The Sickness Unto Death*
C. S. Lewis's *The Abolition of Man*
Saba Mahmood's *The Politics of Piety: The Islamic Revival and the Feminist Subject*
Baruch Spinoza's *Ethics*
Keith Thomas's *Religion and the Decline of Magic*

COMING SOON

Chris Argyris's *The Individual and the Organisation*
Seyla Benhabib's *The Rights of Others*
Walter Benjamin's *The Work Of Art in the Age of Mechanical Reproduction*
John Berger's *Ways of Seeing*
Pierre Bourdieu's *Outline of a Theory of Practice*
Mary Douglas's *Purity and Danger*
Roland Dworkin's *Taking Rights Seriously*
James G. March's *Exploration and Exploitation in Organisational Learning*
Ikujiro Nonaka's *A Dynamic Theory of Organizational Knowledge Creation*
Griselda Pollock's *Vision and Difference*
Amartya Sen's *Inequality Re-Examined*
Susan Sontag's *On Photography*
Yasser Tabbaa's *The Transformation of Islamic Art*
Ludwig von Mises's *Theory of Money and Credit*

Macat Disciplines

Access the greatest ideas and thinkers across entire disciplines, including

Postcolonial Studies

Roland Barthes's *Mythologies*
Frantz Fanon's *Black Skin, White Masks*
Homi K. Bhabha's *The Location of Culture*
Gustavo Gutiérrez's *A Theology of Liberation*
Edward Said's *Orientalism*
Gayatri Chakravorty Spivak's *Can the Subaltern Speak?*

Macat analyses are available from all good bookshops and libraries.

Access hundreds of analyses through one, multimedia tool.
Join free for one month **library.macat.com**

Macat Disciplines

Access the greatest ideas and thinkers across entire disciplines, including

AFRICANA STUDIES

Chinua Achebe's *An Image of Africa: Racism in Conrad's Heart of Darkness*

W. E. B. Du Bois's *The Souls of Black Folk*

Zora Neale Hurston's *Characteristics of Negro Expression*

Martin Luther King Jr.'s *Why We Can't Wait*

Toni Morrison's *Playing in the Dark: Whiteness in the American Literary Imagination*

Macat analyses are available from all good bookshops and libraries.

Access hundreds of analyses through one, multimedia tool.
Join free for one month **library.macat.com**

Macat Disciplines

*Access the greatest ideas and thinkers
across entire disciplines, including*

FEMINISM, GENDER AND QUEER STUDIES

Simone De Beauvoir's
The Second Sex

Michel Foucault's
History of Sexuality

Betty Friedan's
The Feminine Mystique

Saba Mahmood's
*The Politics of Piety:
The Islamic Revival and
the Feminist Subject*

Joan Wallach Scott's
*Gender and the
Politics of History*

Mary Wollstonecraft's
*A Vindication of the
Rights of Woman*

Virginia Woolf's
A Room of One's Own

Judith Butler's
Gender Trouble

 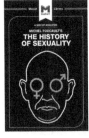  

Macat analyses are available from all good bookshops and libraries.

Access hundreds of analyses through one, multimedia tool.
Join free for one month **library.macat.com**

Macat Disciplines

Access the greatest ideas and thinkers across entire disciplines, including

CRIMINOLOGY

Michelle Alexander's
The New Jim Crow: Mass Incarceration in the Age of Colorblindness

Michael R. Gottfredson & Travis Hirschi's
A General Theory of Crime

Elizabeth Loftus's
Eyewitness Testimony

Richard Herrnstein & Charles A. Murray's
The Bell Curve: Intelligence and Class Structure in American Life

Jay Macleod's
Ain't No Makin' It: Aspirations and Attainment in a Low-Income Neighborhood

Philip Zimbardo's
The Lucifer Effect

Macat Disciplines

Access the greatest ideas and thinkers across entire disciplines, including

INEQUALITY

Ha-Joon Chang's, *Kicking Away the Ladder*

David Graeber's, *Debt: The First 5000 Years*

Robert E. Lucas's, *Why Doesn't Capital Flow from Rich To Poor Countries?*

Thomas Piketty's, *Capital in the Twenty-First Century*

Amartya Sen's, *Inequality Re-Examined*

Mahbub Ul Haq's, *Reflections on Human Development*

Macat Disciplines

Access the greatest ideas and thinkers across entire disciplines, including

GLOBALIZATION

Arjun Appadurai's, *Modernity at Large: Cultural Dimensions of Globalisation*

James Ferguson's, *The Anti-Politics Machine*

Geert Hofstede's, *Culture's Consequences*

Amartya Sen's, *Development as Freedom*

Macat Disciplines

Access the greatest ideas and thinkers across entire disciplines, including

MAN AND THE ENVIRONMENT

The Brundtland Report's, *Our Common Future*
Rachel Carson's, *Silent Spring*
James Lovelock's, *Gaia: A New Look at Life on Earth*
Mathis Wackernagel & William Rees's, *Our Ecological Footprint*

Macat Disciplines
Access the greatest ideas and thinkers across entire disciplines, including

THE FUTURE OF DEMOCRACY

Robert A. Dahl's, *Democracy and Its Critics*
Robert A. Dahl's, *Who Governs?*
Alexis De Toqueville's, *Democracy in America*
Niccolò Machiavelli's, *The Prince*
John Stuart Mill's, *On Liberty*
Robert D. Putnam's, *Bowling Alone*
Jean-Jacques Rousseau's, *The Social Contract*
Henry David Thoreau's, *Civil Disobedience*

Printed and bound by CPI Group (UK) Ltd, Croydon, CR0 4YY

08/06/2025

01896998-0001